THE LOST RAILWAY

THE MIDLANDS

ROBERT DAY

Ian Allan
PUBLISHING

For Dad – E. J. F. 'Ted' Day – whose idea it was

First published 2013

ISBN 978 0 7110 3684 0

© Robert Day 2013

Published by Ian Allan Publishing Ltd, Hersham, Surrey KT12 4RG.

Printed in England

Visit the Ian Allan Publishing website at **www.ianallanpublishing.com**

Photographic Credits
All the photographs in this book are copyright of the author.

FRONT COVER The end wall of Buxton LNWR station. (See also page 58)

BACK COVER Matlock station. (See also page 49)

PREVIOUS PAGE New Mills Central signal box. (See also page 65)

ABOVE Whitchurch signal box. (See also page 82)

Contents

Introduction

There is a railway that we have lost. I'm not referring to closed railways – though there are plenty of those – but rather to a railway that reflected different priorities in business, different ways of working and a different way of life. It was a railway that still hung on to the idea of serving as a universal carrier, that needed the facilities to handle freight, or parcels, just in case a customer in turn needed them. It was a railway where a train still meant some carriages with an engine on the front, or, if it was a multiple unit, it at least had a guard's van for bicycles or the odd bulky package, and on a good day you could sit behind the driver and have the chance of seeing the line from his viewpoint.

This was the railway where stations still had waiting rooms, porters, luggage barrows, stern warning notices that went 'clang' when you threw a stone at them, and gates and fences that were more ornamental than secure. It was the railway where the signals were controlled by a man in a signal box at the end of the platform, and if you wanted to know what was happening to your train you could shout 'Ey up, bobby!' to the box and get an intelligent answer. It was the railway where you could buy a platform ticket for a couple of pence just so that you could have a look around the station without being considered a risk to security.

In short, it was the railway that had served the country well throughout the Age of Steam; and, more to the point, it didn't disappear overnight when steam did.

This book is dedicated to my father, Ted Day, and the story of how we came to do the legwork that led to it is worth telling. Like many men of his generation, Ted served King and Country during the Late Unpleasantness with Germany, and saw active service – in his case, in Palestine and Italy. Having joined the army 'for the duration of the war', he was puzzled when his pay book, together with everyone else's, was withdrawn one day in the field, and was returned 24 hours later with the term 'duration of the war' deleted and 'duration of the emergency' inserted.

This bureaucratic sleight of hand meant that he was not demobbed when the war finished; rather, the Crown retained his services until 1947. He finished his Army career as a drill sergeant training new squaddies at various camps in the rolling land of north-west Nottinghamshire, handy for Dorothy, his new bride, down in Nottingham town itself. Ted was offered his commission, but with the dawning of the Atomic Age he considered (wrongly, as it turned out, but possibly fortunately for me) that the day of the infantryman was over. So he went to seek his fortune in the wide world of post-war Britain. He tried Ericssons at Beeston but, being a straight-talking man, he found he didn't fit in. In need of regular employment, and with my sister on the way, in early 1948 he joined the new British Railways as a permanent way labourer at Toton Yard.

Through sheer native wit, Ted found himself first working with the signal linesmen, then taking the necessary tests to become first assistant linesman, and eventually Toton's chief signalling linesman. The day came when a party of dignitaries came around on an official tour – after all, Toton was one of the showpiece automated marshalling yards of British Railways – and Ted took over giving these dignitaries the Grand Tour, with technical explanations and fielding questions.

Afterwards, the inspector who was in charge of the party collared Ted.

'What's your name, then?' he asked.

'Ted Day,' was the answer.

'Well,' came the reply, 'so why haven't I ever seen your name on any applications for promotion?'

Ted made some sort of excuse, but the inspector left with strict instructions that my father should consider his position when the time came.

A couple of weeks later, Ted was on nights, but he clocked on one evening to be met by his oppo, who said, 'I'm taking your shift – go home and get to bed. Oh, and get your best suit out.'

'Why?' said Dad.

'Because this,' said his mate, waving a memo, 'came for you today. You're to report to Derby Nelson Street tomorrow morning at 10am.'

This left Ted nonplussed. He couldn't think of anything he'd done so wrong that he should be summoned to Derby for a carpeting in front of the higher-ups.

The following morning found him at the Nelson Street offices of the Chief Signalling Engineer. He reported to the designated room, to find a secretary there, typing. 'Oh yes, Mr. Day,' she said. 'They've got someone in with them just now, so if you'll just take a seat they won't be very long.' In due course, someone came out from the inner office, then Ted was told to go in – only to be faced with three managers sitting at a table, one of whom was the inspector who had brought the party of dignitaries around Toton. They invited Ted to be seated and, sensing that he was still a bit bewildered, asked him, 'Do you know why you're here this morning?' When he admitted that he didn't, they told him that he was being interviewed for an opening in the signalling drawing office at Derby.

He was appointed to the post. He now had to learn the theory behind the practical stuff he'd been installing and mending and renewing for the past few years, but again, as a quick learner, he rose to the occasion. Eventually he became involved in the planning and commissioning of new signalling schemes, the main one of which was the resignalling that accompanied the electrification of the first section of the West Coast Main Line and the rebuilding of Euston.

Towards the end of 1966 two things happened. First, there was talk about relocating the signalling drawing office – but to where? Some said Nottingham, others said Birmingham, and there was some talk of Glasgow. Then, one evening, Ted's boss popped his head round the office door and asked him to do a rush job – an hour's overtime was offered. This rush job was to prepare the signalling alterations for the closure of

the Midland line through the Peak from Matlock to Buxton, and the singling of the line from Ambergate to Matlock. Ted was not happy. 'In one hour's overtime,' he later said, 'I put 50 blokes out of work.' And the prospects for the future were not much better. The West Coast electrification north of Weaver Junction was indefinitely postponed, and all the talk was of line closures. My father was faced with the prospect of spending his time taking stuff out, not putting new stuff in. This offended him, and in the new year he applied for and secured a job as a draughtsman with Vic Hallam of Langley Mill. Vic Hallam had started out after the war making chicken houses for back yards and allotments; by the mid-1960s the company had expanded into modular buildings for schools, clinics, hospitals and other public buildings.

One upshot of this was that Ted had to pass his driving test, as the journey from Belper, where we lived, to Langley Mill was a tortuous one by public transport. He'd been driving since he was 14, and had driven in the Army, but like so many others had never passed a driving test – and hadn't needed to, having a railwayman's travel perks that gave him and his immediate family access to a pre-Beeching railway system that went almost everywhere you might want to go. But that was changing, too, so he passed his test and bought a car – a green Morris Oxford, registration YRC 918. We had our first family holiday by car in 1967, touring Norfolk. Then the following year we went to North Wales, and at the age of 11 I discovered the narrow gauge railways of the Principality. We had gone from the railway being a central part of our family life – visiting relatives in Nottingham or London, as well as family holidays – to it not figuring in our lives at all. Suddenly I discovered something that I was missing.

Our trip to North Wales quickly led to our discovering, by chance, that one of my Mum's former bosses had sold his electrical retail business and retired to run a holiday home at Talsarnau, along the

Cambrian Coast line north of Harlech. So we found ourselves going to North Wales on a more frequent basis, and I took along my Kodak Brownie 127 to record what we saw. And increasingly we were seeing mainly railways, and I was photographing them. In 1970 my birthday present was a 'proper' camera – a 35mm Yashica rangefinder model. Then one day Dad heard that the coaling plant at Nottingham shed was due to be demolished, and he said to me that we should photograph it before it was too late.

We were too late. But then he said to me, 'There's all sorts of stuff being taken out that we should record before it's gone,' so we set out to record the railway infrastructure – stations, signal boxes, level crossings, mechanical signals and all the paraphernalia that went with the traditional railway. All the way through the 1970s we recorded this wherever we went; many of our holidays were planned around photographing sections of line, such as the Settle & Carlisle, the Cambrian Coast and many others. In 1975 I went to college in Newcastle-upon-Tyne, and used the benefits of a half-price student railcard to get out and photograph some more railways. As we moved into the 1980s the opportunities changed; the tide of modernisation and gentrification was overtaking smaller stations, closing many and reducing many more to unstaffed halts, with all the 'benefits' that economic stringency brings – neglect, vandalism and disuse.

At the end of the 1970s the economic conditions meant that Dad lost his job at Vic Hallam's, but he was headhunted by a previous client, so Ted and Dorothy moved to North Warwickshire. In 1984 I moved to the area as well, ironically regularly passing the British Rail offices in Birmingham to which the signal drawing office had finally moved from Derby. This meant that we could now photograph some of the stations in the south and west Midlands, though it was something of a race against time to see buildings before they were modernised, brought into line with the new corporate brandings, or just plain demolished as costing too much to maintain. Privatisation in 1989 brought my photography of the main-line railway almost to a full stop, as stations were now no longer temples to public transport and public service, but more and more part of Corporate Britain, to be treated as assets whose secrets needed guarding, and which were now private property. Photography was now discouraged, because of the risk that photographers were stealing intellectual assets and other things that were subject to commercial confidentiality. The security concerns of the new century added to this paranoia – but that's another story.

In the meantime, I turned my photographic attention to Europe, where wiser heads and a tradition of public service persisted. And that, too, is another story.

Ted died in 2000, saddened by the turn that Britain's railways had taken under privatisation. So this book and those that follow are not only dedicated to him, but are also a memorial to his generation and all the other generations of railwaymen who had built a community dedicated to serving the public and transporting them, and their goods and chattels, as safely as possible from A to B. When Ted first started at Toton, there were still old Midland men working there; later, when he had moved to Derby, he often took his lunch in the loco works canteen. In both cases he was impressed with the sense of continuity this gave him. Derby Works had been building and repairing engines since 1840, and that sense of community came down to Ted in a very real way. That sense of community is now considered obsolete and uneconomic; many employers have no sense of loyalty to their employees, and the employees reciprocate. Derby loco works is no more: some of the buildings have found a new use as the campus for Derby College, but I last saw it before this change took place, so all I saw was a few isolated buildings in the middle of a vast retail park; I remember giving thanks that Ted wasn't alive to see the reduction of a proud tradition to a few remains with no obvious connection to their original function. Our country is the poorer for this impoverishment of the working relationship; I hope that this book will be a link to a better time.

Chapter One

CLOSE TO HOME

When my father moved to Derby in 1959, having been headhunted to the signalling drawing office, he decided we should move to within easy commuting distance. Having been born and raised on a farm, he was never a town boy, so he looked at how far out from Derby we could live and still be within concessionary commuting distance. The answer was Belper, a mill town in the Derwent valley, and once notorious as the Parliamentary constituency of George Brown, Harold Wilson's Foreign Secretary in the 1960s Labour Government. We lived out of town at Bargate, a 1920s ribbon development on top of a high sandstone ridge to the east of Belper, with spectacular views to the Chevin, a local hill on the far side of the valley, which might be considered the real start of the Pennine Way. Although Bargate was a good mile out of Belper, and quite a steep hike, Ted would walk up and down to the station each day to commute into Derby, seven miles distant.

For occasions when we made family excursions into Derby, though, we used the bus. The Trent No 90 bus route ran past the front door, connecting Belper and Derby via the villages of Holbrook (where I went to primary school) and Little Eaton. And this was especially important whenever we went away to visit family, or on holiday. Mum's side of the family was in Nottingham, but Dad's relations were still down in his native Essex, nearly at the end of the Central Line in Loughton. So for the first eight years of my time in Belper any long journey started with a bus ride to Derby's 1930s bus station, then either a long walk down Siddals Lane past the paint factory to Derby station or, if we were especially lumbered with luggage, a ride on one of Derby's trolleybuses.

Derby, home of the Midland, including Derby Works and Litchurch Lane

The Derby Midland station I remember was a gloriously ornate affair, befitting the headquarters of the Midland Railway. Once past the ticket barrier with its folding scissor gates, however, you were in a different world, one of brick and concrete, as the old overall roof at Derby Midland had taken a direct hit from a German bomb during the Second World War. The damage was never repaired, British Railways preferring the modernity of low-rise brick and concrete to an early Victorian cast-iron roof, no matter how historic or distinctive. The problem, of course, was that the new materials had nothing like the lasting powers of the old, and very quickly the platform canopies and waiting rooms began to look tatty and dated. Journeys to London inevitably started from Platform 6, the furthest one from the entrance,

which meant a long trek across the footbridge, to be rewarded with the sight of Derby Locomotive Works with its distinctive clock tower and the long access footbridge for staff. Only later did I become aware of the Carriage & Wagon Works, on the other side of London Road and not easily visible from any train, even if we were heading towards the south-west (which to be honest we very rarely did).

Both works held annual open days, ostensibly to show off the products of the various horticultural and other clubs attached to these factories, but as much to throw open their gates to the railway-minded population of Derby and further afield. These were opportunities to see what was in the works, what was new and (sometimes) what was old and on the way out. Open days were great family occasions, and if

The frontage of Derby Midland station, seen here in August 1972, was a grand affair dating from 1893 to reflect the values of the Midland Railway, whose headquarters this was. Derby was one of the earliest major stations in the country; the three constituent companies of the Midland (the North Midland Railway, the Midland Counties Railway and the Birmingham & Derby Junction Railway) pooled their resources to construct a truly magnificent station. This portico, designed by Charles Trubshaw, concealed Francis Thompson's original 1840 station, itself considered to be a magnificent edifice. Some elements of Thompson's original frontage were reused in the new construction. There was a range of administrative buildings all along the length of Midland Road as far as the

corner where Siddals Road began, but in the early 1970s BR demolished the old Midland Railway Traffic Superintendent's offices to create a station car park, hence the gap in the range of buildings to the left of the main block. Over the centre of the portico can be seen the clock, with the Midland's pet heraldic beast, the Wyvern, surmounting it. When the station was redeveloped, the clock and the Wyvern were moved to the car park. To the right of the picture is the Midland Hotel, while outside the station is one of Derby Corporation's Daimler CVG6s (No 155) waiting for business. Meanwhile, the driver of the Rover 2000 seems to be entertaining dreams of starring in *The Sweeney* – or did all cars corner like that in the 1970s?

you look at the pictures I took through the 1970s and 1980s you'll see as many wives, girlfriends and family groups as you will spotters. At its height in 1920 the Works employed 20,000 men; by the time I was taking photographs the combined workforce of the Loco and Carriage & Wagon works was about 7,000, still a significant number. Derby was very definitely a railway town, and the town repaid that compliment at every possible occasion.

The railway route out of Derby with which I was more familiar in those days was the line towards Sawley Junction and the legendary Trent station, at which trains could arrive and depart in almost any direction, not necessarily related to their eventual destination. But first one passed by the loco depot, then seemingly endless rows of condemned coaches before passing a large tract of open waste ground with Chaddesden Sidings visible in the distance, marked only by a deep gully with a stream in the bottom of it and a Hall's Distemper advert hoarding, made famous by the 1930s Hornby/Dinky Toys figures. I only ever remember using the Chaddesden Loop once to enter the station at the north end; little did I know that that was the original route into Derby from the south, and the direct line to Spondon was a later addition.

A reverse angle on the main building, taken on the same day, shows that the building is actually symmetrical. Now we can see the frontage of the Midland Hotel. Although the hotel dates from the opening of the original station – indeed, it is said to be the first railway hotel outside London – it has been added to considerably over the years. It was also designed by Francis Thompson, but erected on the initiative of the contractor who built the station, Thomas Jackson; he ran it until he went bankrupt in 1859. The hotel then passed to a Mrs Julia Ann Blunt, but the Midland Railway board had accepted that good hotels near its stations were a necessity in 1860, and accordingly bought the hotel for £10,050 two years later. We can see clearly the covered way from the station so that guests wouldn't get wet. There's a good view into the taxi rank here, and also a variety of what would now be called classic vehicles parked in the forecourt and elsewhere. The Hillman Minx in the corner of the car park reminds us that in times gone by, car manufacturers didn't change the styling of their products very often; although we can't see the year suffix on the numberplate, it would not have been that old a vehicle, but it was recognisably the same model of car that had gone into production in the 1950s. Just in front of the Minx, on the corner of the entrance to the forecourt, can be seen a Midland Railway boundary marker plate.

Once inside the covered taxi rank, you would have been faced with two halls: arrivals on the left and departures on the right, where the ticket office was situated. This was originally the 3rd Class booking hall, so the finish inside wasn't quite as ornate as the outside, but it was light and pleasant enough. (There was a separate 1st Class ticket hall south of this one, out of use by this time.) In this April 1978 view the ticket windows are out of the picture to the right, while at the end of the hall can be seen the booth installed for the ticket collection staff, and the folding scissor gates. On the left is the W. H. Smith bookstall; the tables in the foreground would take overflow stocks of books or magazines when larger numbers of passengers were expected.

The Smith's bookstall itself was quite a grand affair, with counters serving both halls. It was also a product of the reconstruction in 1955. The traditional station bookstall was not based around a business model which involved customers browsing: you asked for the title you wanted, paid, and were given it. End of transaction. Of course, this also meant that magazine covers were fairly bland things, as they didn't have to entice casual buyers to pick that issue up. The publishers just assumed that their customers bought each copy as it came out.

Given that the 'browsing permitted' model of shop design is so universal nowadays, it comes as a surprise to find places where this isn't the case. I saw a station bookstall in Wroclaw, Poland a couple of years ago which still worked on the old principle - you asked for the title you wanted and the kiosk inhabitant gave it to you in exchange for a few zlotys pushed through a slot. Indeed, it went further than the traditional British open bookstall, in that it looked more like a traditional post office counter, with grilles.

ABOVE Once through the ticket barriers, we are onto the platforms, and things take a turn for the worse. Derby originally had a fine covered train shed, but this took a direct hit from a German bomb on 15 January 1941; there were six fatalities. Travellers had to put up with a 100-yard (92-metre) gap in the overall roof of the train shed until this range of concrete canopies was built in 1952. By the mid-1970s they were looking rather shabby, and in this April 1978 view things are not improved by a heavy rainstorm. The canopies soldiered on until 2005, when replacement work on the footbridge revealed severe deterioration of the concrete. Demolition started in 2007 and new steel canopies were completed in 2009.

Then, as now, Derby had six platforms; Platform 6, as well as being the departure platform for services to London, gave a

panoramic view of the Loco Works yard. Although the concrete canopies did not age well, they did at least allow a good amount of light down onto the platforms.

BELOW Also to be seen in the arrivals hall – increasingly less often used as the 1970s went on – was this memorial to Midland Railway staff who lost their lives in the Boer War. The memorial, which commemorates staff from all over the system, not just from Derby, records the names of 55 Army reservists and 13 members of the Militia, Yeomanry and volunteers. When Derby station was reconstructed in 1985, this plaque, together with others from within Derby Works, was restored and relocated to Platform 1.

The more southerly footbridge afforded this fine vista of the platforms at Derby. This August 1972 view
shows five – yes, count them, five! – trains in the station at once. Platform 5 was a bay at the south end
of Platforms 4 and 6, and can be seen on the extreme right of this picture; it could hold a two-car DMU.
This picture also shows well the platform side of the range of station buildings; you can get a good idea
of the extent of them, fully a thousand feet long. You can also see the typical paraphernalia of a 1970s
railway station with various stepladders, buckets and platform trolleys littered around, the backs of
a couple of colour light signals, and spotters. Plenty of spotters! In the 1970s this activity was not
unfashionable. The group on the end of Platforms 2 and 3 are obviously there for the afternoon,
and they are causing nobody any trouble. I wonder if any of those in this picture are still enthusiasts,
40 years on?

ABOVE Although Derby power signal box came into use in 1969 and nearly all the mechanical signal boxes around the station were demolished as a consequence, one traditional signal box survived. This was Engine Sidings No 2, seen here on the same occasion in August 1972. It controlled the yard entry to the works at the south end of the station, and was the newest Midland-era signal box at Derby, having been commissioned in 1890. Engine Sidings No 1 was at the opposite end of the Loco Works yard, but by the time this picture was taken it had been reduced to a ground frame that was unlocked from Engine Sidings No 2 (though retaining its name). No 2 carried on until 1987. Of interest is the signalman's coal bunker by the foot of the stairs, by this time reduced to a glorified rubbish dump as the box has had a gas supply put in – the gas pipe can be seen running up the end wall of the box, and the signal box chimney has an appropriate cowling. Visible in the background is the Derby Works water softening plant, dating from 1928, which had the benefit of a pair of Fowler tenders as water bowsers.

RIGHT Here we can see the 1840 clock tower during the 1980 Works Open Day. As I said earlier, the open days were big occasions in Derby and, given the sunshine, lots of people have turned out for this one, accessing the works via the 'clerk's footbridge' from outside the station. This block of buildings has been much altered over the years; originally single-storey, a first floor was added in 1859 and a second in 1893. In 1950 a fire resulted in serious damage to the top floor, and repairs were made in the contemporary style, which then stood out like a very sore thumb; when the block was renovated in 2007 to form part of the Derby College campus, the opportunity was taken to remake those repairs in a more sympathetic style. The clock is original, and was made by John Whitehurst of Derby; the tower also housed a bell said to be taken from the old St Pancras chapel in London when that building was demolished in 1865 to make way for St Pancras station; it bears the date 1717.

LEFT The interior of the 1840 Roundhouse No 1, a rare Francis Thompson survivor, is seen here in September 1977. Through the 1970s and 1980s this was used for the repair and maintenance of cranes. Now also incorporated into the Derby College campus as a cafeteria, the Roundhouse has also hosted the Derby Real Ale Festival.

RIGHT The entrance to the Roundhouse was flanked by two war memorial tablets commemorating those from this specific shop who served in the First World War. Sixty-one names are recorded, of whom 15 did not return. Here is one of the plaques, photographed in September 1980, with an old shell case serving as a flower vase. Many of the individual shops within the Loco Works had their own memorial plaques, and the reverence shown them was another example of the continuity of community that could be found within Derby Works. These plaques have now been relocated to the station, as described above.

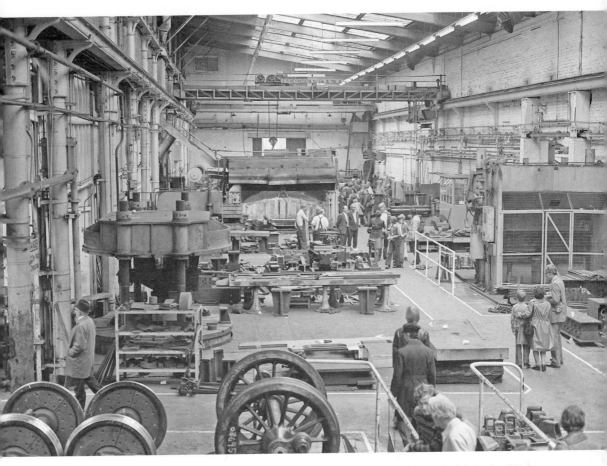

The Flanging Shop was photographed during the 1977 Open Day; visible on the left is a 500-ton wheel press, installed in 1913, and in the background is a furnace, capable of reaching temperatures of up to 900° Celsius. Works managers, not to mention the trade union health and safety representative, would have apoplexy at the lack of guards, warning notices and other safety measures to which we have become accustomed – and not a hard hat or hi-visibility jerkin anywhere to be seen!

ABOVE This view of the former Wheel & Tyre Shop shows well the overhead crane, built by Craven Bros in Manchester in 1892. Although locomotive construction ceased at Derby in 1966, the facilities were invaluable for heavy repairs and overhauls.

LEFT And as for the proximity of the public to this hot work – well, perhaps this is a lack of health and safety gone mad!

Originally the Erecting Shop, No 8 Shop was used for all repair work; it had been brought into service in 1873 as part of the expansion programme for the works. It was 450 feet long and 325 feet across, and consisted of seven bays which could accommodate (in steam days) up to 108 locomotives at one time. Once engine building ceased at Derby, the works were put over entirely to repairs and overhauls; in 1977, we see here HST power cars being rotated through the Works, though more traditional London Midland Region visitors can be seen on the adjacent road in the form of a number of Class 45s.

Having said that locomotive construction ceased in 1966, Derby Works did have a swansong, albeit an inglorious one. In 1980 Derby constructed the six power cars for the Advanced Passenger Train pre-production prototypes (ATP-P). Some idea of the problems encountered with this project can be gauged from the fact that the driving trailers and coaches were being turned out two years earlier. Here is one of the power cars, No 49003, undergoing static testing in No 7 Shop in September 1980. Photography was supposedly not allowed in this area, but no one seemed to be enforcing this prohibition. As one of the 'flagship' batch of power cars, No 49003 bore the name City of Derby. Derby was only made a city in 1977, so this was be the first time that a Derby-built 'engine' could bear this name, and it turned out to be the last. So it's ironic that, had the APT entered service, it would have been unlikely that this nameplate would ever have been seen in its native city. Derby has always been off the map as far as electrification proposals were concerned, although Norman Fowler's 1981 report into railway electrification (commissioned by the previous Callaghan Government) might have seen Derby wired up by 1990 (if work had started immediately on publication!). Local MPs regularly call for the St Pancras to Bedford electrification to be extended to Sheffield, and in fact this has finally been recommended as part of the 2012 infrastructure plan.

ABOVE It's now time for a look at the Carriage & Wagon Works across the way. Work commenced on building these Works in 1874, and it was fully completed in 1877. Before that date, carriages and wagons had been built and maintained in part of the main Locomotive Works on the far side of the station. This picture, from 1978, shows 'U' Shop (formerly known as the Lifting Shop), which was built in 1910 as part of the modernisation of the Works. Just visible behind the visitors on the extreme right of the picture is a board showing typical components of the different bogies in use at that time; there are separate sections for the new B4-B5 bogies, Commonwealth, BR and LMS examples.

RIGHT Litchurch Lane Works was not as photogenic as the Locomotive Works, but it did have its items of interest, such as the traversers. The power units for the traversers were essentially 0-4-0 locomotives; the originals resembled steam tram locomotives, but from 1911 onwards these were replaced by electric units with overhead pick-ups, built on the original chassis, but housed in what can only be described as a shed with trolley poles. One of these units has had an extension of life after being declared redundant, as it was acquired by the Great Western Society and moved to its Didcot site, where it was installed outside the carriage shed (and painted chocolate and cream by some philistine, though I'm told it has now been repainted into something more like BR carmine and cream).

RIGHT Seen here in May 1977, this range of offices on the south side of the station on Nelson Street was built in 1872-73. The later building, which housed Ted's signalling drawing office, was originally the location of the Midland's Goods Manager, but the earlier of the two was the Chief Accountant's office from the time of its construction up to at least the time of this picture, some 105 years later!

BELOW The railway community in Derby consisted of more than just the station and the two works. A small railway village was built around the station from the outset, consisting of railway workers' houses, hotels, workshops, the Signalling Works and various other offices. We have already seen the Midland Hotel; here is the official Midland Railway war memorial. Designed, like the Cenotaph in London, by Sir Edwin Lutyens, it backs onto the garden of the Midland Hotel.

RIGHT Opposite the station was the bulk of the Railway Institute, one of those great monuments to self-improvement of the working man. Starting with the humble origins of a group of employees who met in the nearby Brunswick Tavern and founded a Reading Society in 1850, this establishment contained meeting rooms, classrooms, a concert hall with seating for 500, and a notable library with more than 14,000 volumes, the railway titles of which eventually found their way into the hands of the Midland Railway Trust. It was designed and built at the same time as the covered portico to the station (1894), and was also the work of Charles Trubshaw. By the time I knew it in the early 1970s some concessions to entertainment had been made, such as the installation of some bars and its formal incorporation as Branch 105 of the BR Staff Association. Meetings of the Midland Railway Project Group, the preservationists who eventually created the Midland Railway Centre at Butterley, took place here for many years. The building has now been transformed into an upmarket bar with function rooms, though the concert hall remains unused; local theatre groups are attempting to restore it to its former use.

BELOW The North Midland Railway built a settlement of workers' houses immediately opposite its new station in 1840. Over the years these were expanded, and other workshops and establishments sprang up in the area.

This is Leeds Place, just next to the Railway Institute, and this May 1977 picture shows the Midland Railway's ticket printing office. Tickets were printed here from 1844 until May 1934, when the LMS transferred all ticket printing to Euston. The premises passed to a number of other owners, eventually reverting to printing work with a local company, J. H. Hall & Sons. The building was eventually demolished during the renovation of the area in 1982.

ABOVE And this is one block of the 1840 NMR housing on Railway Terrace – solid, well-proportioned workers' accommodation, designed again by Francis Thompson. These properties, being closest to the station, were occupied by officers, foremen and other senior staff, some of which were 'on call' via a bell installed in the houses. This section has been restored over recent years and these streets are now a conservation area.

Midland Place ran parallel to Railway Terrace, and consisted of more workers' housing; being further from the station, these cottages were occupied by less exalted officers and staff. Opposite the houses, William Bemrose set up his printing works, producing a stream of timetables, stationery and publicity leaflets for the railway.

BELOW And on the corner we see here in 1977 the Loco Sports Club. Interestingly, when Ted took this picture in May 1977 it was just a few months after the building was officially listed as being of architectural and/or historical importance. Though the area didn't show it when these pictures were taken, others were recognising the importance of the whole range of railway buildings in Derby and laying the groundwork for the conservation of this area.

ABOVE But there was another locus to the Midland Railway's activities in Derby. This was St Mary's Goods Yard, a massive area that ran alongside the Chesterfield Road, all the way from St Mary's Bridge to Little Chester and beyond. Powers to construct the goods branch were sought in the same Act that authorised the construction of the Ripley branch, but the first stage of the extensive goods facility opened in 1855. Work continued to expand this facility to meet the ever-increasing goods traffic until 1868. Generally a closed book to the average citizen – in this July 1973 view, you can see the high wall that shielded goods activity from the prying eyes of the public – most people hardly noticed as this installation gradually lost traffic and eventually fell derelict. In 1992 the site was acquired for the relocation of the headquarters of the Prison Service from London to Derby, and work started on clearing the site. Then, on 16 September that year, the Government was forced to withdraw the pound sterling from the European monetary exchange rate mechanism, and in the emergency austerity measures imposed by the Treasury in the aftermath of what became known as 'Black Wednesday' the project was cancelled at a cost of some £30 million. Derby lost some 2,000 jobs, which would have followed the relocation, and the contractor was awarded some £9 million in cancellation fees. The cleared site was eventually put to new housing, although some of the goods buildings have been listed and put to other uses.

LEFT This view of the north end of the St Mary's Goods Yard complex, taken in March 1973, gives some idea of the extent of the yard. The goods sheds can be seen in the background. The Goods Yard Box isn't in the easiest of locations to photograph without trespassing, but this view has items of interest. The box itself is an LMS standard timber box, built at some point after 1928. We also get a good view of a large number of short-armed shunting signals; two posts with two shunting arms, one post facing each way at the entrance to the yard; and five posts on the LMS-era Pratt 'N' truss gantry.

Attenborough

Although the biggest railway adventures of that time were our trips to London, with wonders to behold such as the ability of the catering stewards on the train to pour coffee and milk simultaneously from the long-spouted pots into the cups with unerring accuracy, Wellingborough shed, the Weetabix factory at Burton Latimer, the seemingly endless brick-lined cuttings on the approach to St Pancras, followed by the sight of the famous gasometers and the coach for the training of catering staff permanently stabled in their shadow, and finally the arrival in the stupendous train shed of St Pancras itself, just as interesting a trip was the shorter excursion to see Mum's family in Nottingham and district. If we were going to see Uncle Winston – who had at one time been a fireman at Nottingham shed before the lure of driving a forklift at the Boots company's infamous 'Beeston fog works' for more money proved too strong a temptation – then we would detrain at Attenborough.

Opened as a roadside halt in 1864, Attenborough has surprisingly long platforms and quite an extensive platform building, considering that it only serves a dormitory suburb of Nottingham. Except that there is more to it than that. Ten minutes' walk up the road brings you to Chilwell's National Shell Filling factory, which from October 1916 was one of the main munitions factories in the country (not to be confused with the Royal Ordnance Factory in Nottingham itself). At opening, the factory employed 6,000 people; by the end of the First World War this had risen to 10,000. Between 1936 and 1940 the site became a major depot for the Royal Army Ordnance Corps and later the Royal Engineers, being simply known locally as 'Chilwell Depot'. It was at that time a major depot for motor transport and spares. It was rail-connected between Attenborough and Trent, hence the rather more substantial signal box and the longer platforms to handle peak flows of personnel; in 1915 the station had handled 34,000 passengers in the year, but the following year this rose to 84,000. From the Second World War until the 1960s additional passenger trains ran from Mansfield and Newark to accommodate workers who lived further afield. These trains ran directly into the depot to a newly built dedicated covered platform, and did not appear in the public timetable. Most of the depot and all its railway operations closed at the end of March 1982.

The pictures date from a warm but wet afternoon in July 1973.

FACING PAGE This is the platform building on the Nottingham-bound platform, erected during the First World War. This supplemented an earlier building further along the platform in the direction of Trent, which had disappeared by the time this picture was taken in 1973; its location is marked by the patch of grass behind the far lamp-post. The two rather functional toilet blocks at each end of the building are original, though comparison with contemporary photographs shows that the windows in the block nearest the camera are later additions. That block contained facilities for ladies and gents (the Chilwell ordnance factory employed very large numbers of women); the one at the far end of the building appears to have been a gents only. By the time the photograph was taken, the nearer block was apparently not in use. Interestingly, the Midland platform seat visible in this picture is also in the archive photograph I consulted – so it had been on the same platform for nearly 60 years. I can be reasonably confident in making this statement, as it appears to have been the only seat on this platform other than the bench integral to the building itself!

TOP RIGHT A long-distance express drops its pilot at Attenborough, as engineering works were in progress on this Sunday. Again, the length of the platforms at Attenborough can be seen. The platform shelter on this side of the station is less substantial, suggesting that most of the passengers would travel from and back to Nottingham.

BELOW In this final picture, we get a good view into the signal box itself. Visible through the open window is the frame of the capstan used to open the crossing gates. This signal box is typical Midland from the first floor upwards, but has a substantial brick base. This may well reflect the danger from explosion at Chilwell; on 1 July 1918 eight tons of TNT exploded in the shell-filling factory with a toll of 137 killed and 250 injured. The brick base dates from a later period. The box survived until 1982. The whole station was remodelled in 2005 and now nothing of the original remains apart from the brick towers of the footbridge.

Nottingham

But if we were going to see some of Mum's old friends, then we'd go all the way into Nottingham Midland itself, with its long platforms and girder bridge bisecting the station, carrying the Great Central line on its way to Nottingham Victoria. The journey wasn't quite so luxurious as the London services, as diesel multiple units were introduced on the Derby-Nottingham-Lincoln trains from 1958, but there was certainly enough to see. For a start, you might occasionally be lucky enough to get a seat behind the driver's cab, with the excellent forward view of the track ahead. Then there was the approach to Nottingham itself, with Nottingham Castle high on its hill to the left of the line, and the extensive goods yard below it (later to be replaced by the headquarters of the Inland Revenue). Nottingham Midland's frontage and forecourt was – and still is – an impressive covered structure with ornate gateways at each end, through which Nottingham's licensed cabs, with their distinctive black bodywork and white bonnet and boot lids, would come and go. Nottingham and Leicester Midland were cut from the same cloth, at street level at least.

In these appallingly murky pictures, taken from the Wilford Road bridge on a grey (and later wet) Sunday in April 1975, we are looking south towards Beeston and the site of Nottingham loco shed – the cleared area on the other side of the running lines. Still in place is the goods yard, though this is rapidly filling up with wagons that were being withdrawn as wagonload freight declined. And not only wagons: the early containers that fitted on the traditional four-wheeled wagon chassis – 'Conflats' – were also being withdrawn as the larger, standard ISO 20-foot and 40-foot containers were becoming more widespread. In this picture, there are various Speedlink containers on Conflats awaiting their next duty, which may not come. Just visible on the right of the picture is the jib of a Coles mobile crane, which would have been used to transfer those containers to flatbed lorries for onward delivery. The tank wagon (bottom right) has been reduced to Departmental use and carries a restricted routing notice, which sadly is unreadable beneath many years of oil spillage from the filler cap. And for all those who remember the British Trix 'Speedfreight' Conflat wagon, one of the prototype containers sits in the foreground awaiting its fate.

ABOVE There was still a sign of the past – the bonded warehouse still carried LMS lettering.

BELOW This is the imposing frontage of Nottingham Midland station, designed by local architect A. E. Lambert and completed in 1904. This picture was taken from Carrington Street; the road going off to the left is Station Street, and the earlier station that this one replaced faced onto that road (hence the name). Lambert had designed the Great Central's grand station at Nottingham Victoria (now almost completely vanished) four years before, and the Midland board was very conscious that their old station looked decidedly shabby by comparison. Leicester station had been remodelled in 1895 but, despite knowing about the Great Central's plans for its new station in Nottingham since 1897, no decision was taken on the fate of the Midland station until 1902. The first contract for the new station – to the same design as Leicester – was let in January 1903, and in six days less than a year the station was completed and opened to passengers! Note the rather attractive Art Deco gates on the Station Street end of the covered taxi rank, and the 'MR' in the terracotta brickwork above the archway. The clock tower is an ornate yet rather squat affair.

ABOVE The portico at the opposite end of the taxi rank also has ornate brick mouldings over the archway, but this time no 'MR' – this portico faces 'out of town', so the need to impress was diminished.

ABOVE Trains leaving Nottingham for the east pass by a rather impressive parcels depot, on the left in the direction of travel. This building has a complex and fascinating history, as it served as another station – Nottingham London Road – until 1944. London Road was built by the grandly named Ambergate, Nottingham & Boston & Eastern Junction Railway, which, like so many of the early railways, had a name that was almost longer than the line it built! In this case, the intention of the company, to link the Midland's Derby-Manchester line with Lincolnshire, was realised only in that it completed the line to from Nottingham to Grantham before leasing the route to the Great Northern Railway in 1855. The company sunk most of its resources into constructing this rather grand terminus building, which opened in 1857, but also served as the company's offices right up to the Grouping of 1923 (albeit only as a 'brass plaque' operation after the lease to the GNR took effect in 1860). The building was designed by another local architect, T. C. Hine, who was responsible for the remodelling of Nottingham Castle in 1867-68. It saw a lot of passenger traffic, especially when the LNWR started services over its joint line with the GNR from Market Harborough and Northampton in 1879. At that time London Road saw up to 80 passenger trains a day during the week, with extra services at weekends. However, after the Great Central opened its Victoria station in 1900 and came to an arrangement with the Great Northern to share it, traffic went into a decline. London Road closed to passenger traffic in 1944, the LNWR Northampton trains being diverted into Victoria; after that it saw further use as a parcels depot, in which form we see it here. It has since been restored as a health centre.

RIGHT Nottingham Midland possessed six platforms, and was notable for being traversed by the 170 feet (52 metres) of the Great Central's bowstring girder bridge. At the time of my visit Platform 6 was fenced off and out of use; it had been in this condition since 1969, when Trent power box opened and the goods avoiding lines to the south of the station were removed. Platform 6 subsequently became the Up Goods line. However, during the 1970s increasing football excursion traffic (probably due to the success of Nottingham Forest under the managership of Brian Clough from 1975 onwards) put strain on the facilities at Nottingham, and it was decided to reopen Platform 6 for that traffic. Indeed, the Football Association provided funding towards the cost of reinstating the passenger facilities on the platform. Football excursions have long since ceased, but the additional capacity proved so useful that Platform 6 has since been re-integrated into the normal operations of the station. The cast-iron roof supports for the extensive canopy were made by Handyside & Co of Derby. Because of the length of the platforms, each platform face could accommodate two trains, made workable by scissors crossovers midway along each platform and controlled by signal boxes on those platforms. However, on that Sunday in April 1975 the weather was so poor that all the camera yielded were mostly pictures of long, empty platforms. At least I was able to photograph this interesting platform barrow, of unknown origin.

Belper

My home town was Belper, in the Derwent Valley. Mainly notable for its huge mill, George and Robert Stephenson drove the North Midland Railway through here in 1839. To keep the line well clear of the flood plain of the Derwent, they adopted a lengthy cutting, lined with ashlar stone blocks, through the middle of the town. This meant that the company had to provide a considerable number of overbridges to accommodate the various streets of the town – ten bridges in less than a mile.

I went to school in Belper from 1969 onwards, attending an establishment founded in 1909 by the Strutt family, the local mill-owners. Although the school backed onto the railway, there was no group of spotters among the pupils. What I do remember was walking to school down Gibfield Lane, over the railway, and seeing mixed freights passing along the line. My school, the Herbert Strutt Grammar School, was one of those establishments that aped the manners and style of a public school, though to its credit it did provide a number of notables in British life over the years. I can put my hand on my heart and say that I went to school with James Bond, in the form of the actor Timothy Dalton, and he was merely following in the steps of an earlier Strutter, Alan Bates. But the role of this school is best summed up in this story, which I had from Chris Moncrieff, the Press Association's long-standing Parliamentary Correspondent (and himself a native of Ilkeston), which concerned George Brown, who we have encountered already.

By birth, Brown was a Man of the People, and always had a great contempt for those whom he considered to have had a privileged upbringing. So when, as Foreign Secretary, some problem or other was kicking off in the Middle East, he was very dubious when his Foreign Office officials suggested that they get in their 'Man on the Spot' to give Brown a briefing on the current situation.

Expecting a chinless wonder from the Home Counties, Brown was on his guard when this wunderkind was ushered into his office, and even more so when his first words were, 'Ah, Foreign Secretary – my father will be so pleased to hear that I've met you.'

Suspecting some classic Eton or Oxbridge social ploy, Brown growled back, 'And just who the hell is your father?', only to be told, 'He opens your carriage door for you on Belper station.' It is a reasonable guess that that FCO expert had, of necessity, been to Strutts.

Belper's original station was located adjacent to the main Derby Road to the south of the town. It later became the site of Belper Goods, while a new station was opened in 1878 on King Street, the main shopping thoroughfare. The booking office was a free-standing building at street level, approached through a fine pair of wrought-iron gates. There was then a fair walk to the separate platforms, located within the cutting through which the line ran through the town. The platforms were shortened during the 1960s and the platform buildings – a pair of stone-built waiting rooms – were removed at the same time. This picture was taken in January 1973.

ABOVE In this July 1977 view, taken from the New Road bridge looking north, the station building seen in the last picture has been replaced by a new supermarket, visible on the next overbridge. This picture gives a good idea of the depth of the cutting and the substantial nature of the rusticated stonework. A path (in Derbyshire dialect, a 'jinnel' or 'jitty') ran between New Road and King Street along the line of the cutting, and rejoiced in the name of 'the Bowling Alley' – quite why is unclear, because there was no record of any such activity in the area. The building with the arched entryway was originally one of the earliest buildings occupied by the Park Foundry, one of Belper's major employers at the time. The company later became well-known for its line of popular gas fires under the trade name 'Parkray'. After it outgrew this rather restricted site, the building became a small council depot and was still in use as such all the way through the 1960s and 1970s.

BELOW This is Belper Goods, looking south in July 1973. The original Francis Thompson station building has vanished completely and subsequent realignments have obliterated any sign of its presence. Belper gasworks was located here, conveniently linked to the railway for the delivery of coal. In the distance can be seen an accommodation bridge (the line crosses the River Derwent between the goods yard and the overbridge, but perspective compresses the view and the river bridge is invisible in this picture). A short distance beyond the overbridge the line plunges into Milford Tunnel; the outline of George Stephenson's sighting tower can just be seen on the skyline, although partially obscured by trees.

The Ripley branch

There was another railway almost as close to home as the Midland main line, but it was rather less grand. This was the Midland branch from Little Eaton to Ripley, which came within two miles or so of our house. (In fact, there was an even closer railway, or more properly tramroad, as a branch from the Little Eaton Gangroad – which the Ripley branch superseded – came via a rope-worked incline to within a few yards of the end of our lane, then on to Belper Pottery, but until recently I had no idea of its existence.) The line opened in 1856; although the passenger service ceased in 1930, the line continued in use all the time I was living at Bargate, for the extraction of coal, first from Denby Colliery then, more recently, for the removal of opencast coal from the area around Denby. Denby also served as a concentration depot for the dwindling number of collieries in the area, though nowadays the name is better known for a popular range of crockery. In the 1960s, '70s and even '80s it was still well-maintained, though it did provide a rich source for the Midland Railway Project Group (later the Midland Railway Trust at Butterley) when its members were recovering signalling equipment for eventual use on their museum line. The course of the line petered out in the vicinity of the remains of Denby Colliery, and disappeared almost completely after the site of Marehay crossing on what used to be the A61 Derby-Chesterfield road. Ripley station remained, however, though disused for many years, and had an ornate Midland Railway terracotta brick panel in one end wall.

The metals are still in place today, which is really rather remarkable, considering the haste with which rails used to be torn up when railways closed in the Beeching era. Even more astonishing is the fact that when the A38 trunk road was upgraded into a full dual carriageway (superseding the A61) the line was given some quite impressive underpasses, even though the line was almost certainly marked down for closure in the 1980s when the dual carriageway was built. There must be some interesting bureaucratic manoeuvring behind the scenes to come out in the telling of that story! When the aforementioned Midland Railway Trust was looking for a suitable museum line in the early 1970s, the Ripley branch was considered for preservation, but later dismissed because of the number of level crossings along its route – six in little more than 4 miles, and seven if there had been sufficient impetus to reclaim the line all the way into Ripley. Eventually, traffic ceased on the line in 1999 and, although theoretically only 'mothballed', the connection to the main line was severed in 2002. Despite all these potential drawbacks, at the end of 2010 a local business partnership proposed reopening the line using EU funding. Whether this comes to fruition remains to be seen.

This July 1973 picture shows some of the area's railway prehistory; the house with the clock once presided over the Little Eaton basin of the Derby Canal, and the open area in front of the house – formerly the agent's office – was taken up with the canal and exchange sidings of the Little Eaton Gangroad. This plateway opened in 1795 and closed in 1908. In the background can be seen the goods shed connected with the Ripley branch, located between the junction with the Midland main line and Little Eaton Station crossing.

ABOVE The signal box at Little Eaton Station crossing was unusual for its reduced height; nonetheless, it possessed a 16-lever frame. However, from March 1969 it ceased to be a block post when the section of line from here back to the main-line junction was reduced to single line and 'one engine in steam' working was introduced. It remained in situ for a number of years serving as a base for a shunter who was carried on the coal trains that still worked up and down the branch and whose duties were to assist the train crew in operating the numerous level crossings on the line. Eventually, the box was replaced by a Portakabin, but the original survives in private ownership. In this view of the crossing gates in 1973, most of the windows have been boarded up, and the staircase has been renewed, omitting the tablet exchange platform that was a feature of a lot of the boxes along this line.

FACING PAGE TOP The next station up the line was Coxbench, long since sold as a private residence. The station building has suffered a change in its fenestration on the platform side; the modernisation of the station master's house is less unsympathetic. This picture dates from Christmas Eve 1977 and was taken from the new A38 dual carriageway; the road in the foreground is the superseded A61. This view gives a good idea of the station's location in the countryside.

FACING PAGE BOTTOM This is Denby Park Hall Crossing signal box, previously known as Denby North. Erected in 1902 to replace an earlier box, it contained a 20-lever frame, as did its companion at Denby South, so you can get a good idea of the complexity of the railway installation here in the line's heyday. After 'one engine in steam' working was introduced in 1968, this box was reduced to the status of a shunting frame. It closed completely in April 1972, and by the time this picture was taken in December 1977 it was all but derelict, but it hung on until at least 1982. The staircase has a tablet exchange platform. The box – and especially its staircase! – looks distinctly off-square; this area has been worked for coal for centuries, and some ground movement may have taken place. The road leads through the spoil tips to a small stone-built manor house, Denby Park Hall. The crossing gates have been crudely replaced with flimsy substitutes dating from the late 1960s.

Only a few yards further on was Denby station itself (originally called Smithy Houses). Considering the length of time that the station had been closed, and the general dereliction of the area, the station building was in quite good condition. Park Hall crossing can be seen in the middle distance in the second photograph, which is taken looking south. On the left of the line can be seen a low platform, dating from the opening of the line in 1856; it incorporated a number of stone sleeper blocks reused from the tramroads in the area. The later, full-height platform opposite brought Denby into line with the other stations in having their single platforms on the same side of the line. The station master's house stands on the same side of the line, a fine solid structure cared for by its new owners. Two Midland gas lamp posts stand at the platform ends, and next to the station master's house is a yard office and the goods shed – both long since sold on for other uses and painted white by their new owner. On the horizon can be seen a row of houses; this was the ridge where the house I grew up in was located, on Sandbed Lane.

The line disappears north of Denby as the landscape has been remodelled extensively following the closure of Denby Colliery. It could be traced for a long time at the site of Marehay crossing but, once on the other side of the A61, more reclamation has taken place which has wiped the landscape clean of any trace of railway. Occasionally one could come across isolated bridges poking out of the landscape, but these often didn't bear too much resemblance to what the Ordnance Survey map suggested ought to be there.

Opened on 2 September 1889 Ripley station replaced an earlier terminus about a mile to the south on the outskirts of the town. Ripley station building remained intact until it was demolished in 1985, 55 years after the regular railway service ceased (although it continued to cater for small goods and ticket sales on an agency basis until 1963, and some excursion traffic for a few years after that). This picture was taken in March 1973. Up on the chimney breast is an ornate working of the letters 'MR' in brickwork.

Langley Mill

When my father left BR in 1966 he went to work, as recounted above, for Vic Hallam's at Langley Mill, just between Heanor and Eastwood on the border between Derbyshire and Nottinghamshire. This was an interesting area for railways, though many of them had been removed or were in advanced stages of decay. The Midland's Erewash Valley main line passed through Langley Mill, though the station closed in 1967 (it was to be reinstated in 1986). Also in the area were a number of lines that the Great Northern had built in the 1870s to tap into the Nottinghamshire coalfield. One of these ran parallel to the Midland line but on the other side of the River Erewash. These lines carried vast quantities of coal and iron products – the GNR handled more than 1.15 million tons of minerals in 1887 at Colwick, east of Nottingham, where there were junctions with the Midland and LNWR lines.

Also at this time at Langley Mill was the Beggarlee branch, a line that started at Langley Mill, connected with Underwood, Brinsley, Selston, Moor Green (last of these to close in 1985), High Park and Watnall New collieries, and finally joined the Midland Bennerley Junction to Bulwell line. It also possessed connections to the Great Northern lines in the area. It was described in the 1937 LMS Sectional Appendix as 'Messrs Barber & Walker's colliery branch', though it was actually in Midland ownership for 35 chains (770 yards/710 metres) up to the point where it made an end-on junction with the Barber & Walker line as well as with the Great Northern Railway's Erewash Valley line. The Barber & Walker line was a well-set-up operation, with workmen's trains, signal boxes and all the paraphernalia of a 'proper' railway, though it had started life at some time before 1836 as a plateway. The company owned and operated mines in the area from as early as 1680; only its workings at Eastwood and Langley Mill lasted into the railway age, the company opening collieries in South Yorkshire when its Nottinghamshire pits became worked out.

The Beggarlee branch ran off the Erewash Valley main line and swung across the Ripley road before entering a small yard. In this sequence of pictures taken in March 1973, the yard was being used by the local Co-op as a coal depot. The first picture shows the delightful ground frame in the transfer yard at Langley Mill, which had been added to by generations of railwaymen to make a comfortable 'bothy' for them to work and rest in. It had probably been there for some time: a study of the point rodding emerging from the ground frame suggests that the carrying rollers had been used for the original round Midland point rodding, and indeed the cranks just visible at the bottom of the picture are just that type, adapted for the much later BR square-section rodding. The timber post carries a rail chair suspended on a length of chain to provide the necessary tension to return the levers to their proper position after use. This frame only worked the sidings immediately adjacent to the junction.

LEFT This picture is looking down the branch, just a few yards from the ground frame; it is protected by a catch point, which itself is protected by an LMS-era tubular steel Home signal. Of interest is the 'Switch' sign, which appears to be of Midland origin; to the right of this, a shunter's pole is leaning up against a fence-post, handy for the next cut of wagons going into or out of the sidings.

ABOVE The line is check-railed here to make sure nothing comes off on the sharp curve through the level crossing. On the left is the ground frame (or, in Midland parlance, a 'stage') that controls the Home signals and the catch points. Attached to the telegraph pole just beyond the ground frame is the apparatus for electrically unlocking the ground frame. In the foreground you can see the Midland-era pulleys for the cable run to the Home signal controlling access to the main line. Looking at the crossing gates themselves, the bar that locks the gates can be clearly seen (painted black). You can also see that the crossing gate target discs are both off-centre; the reason for this is that if you compare the width of the gate with the width of the road, you will see that the gates are not as wide as the road. Indeed, both gates are hinged on the same side, so when closed they only block the road off in one direction. Each gate is only half the width of the road – certainly not the normal arrangement.

LANGLEY MILL & ALDERCAR
CO-OPERATIVE
COAL DEPARTMENT

ABOVE Here is a view of the yard. The painted sign for the Langley Mill & Aldercar Co-op is rather fine. This view shows well the narrowness of the crossing gates. Note the Midland diagonal fencing, behind which is a substantial earth-filled buffer stop, and beyond that another LMS tubular Home signal. Barber & Walker operated workmen's trains from here from at least 1874, using four coaches purchased from the LNWR. In 1946 there were still six workmen's trains per day operating from here to Old Watnall, and one train a day to Selston, and these services continued for a while under the NCB. Given that the wagons in the yard are all internal-user examples and yet contain coal, it is possible that there was still some coal coming out of Moor Green Colliery at this time to meet wholesale orders originating from the Co-op. The line closed in or around March 1984 and the connection to the BR lines was severed, leaving an isolated section used for tipping dirt on the site of Plumtree Colliery until November of that year.

LEFT This is the ground frame. It is very substantially made – you can see why the Midland called them 'stages'. The lever frame itself is an old LNWR Sketch 80 tappet frame. These were used on ground frames by the LMS because they did not require covering against the weather.

RIGHT The crossing was protected by a set of Midland Railway trespass signs. The warning sign is dated 1899, though of course it may have been installed later than that date.

So this was my railway hinterland – the stations I went to and travelled from. Strange to relate, I never travelled north very much at all until I became a student in Newcastle-upon-Tyne, so the railway north of Belper was something of a mystery to me for a long time. But that's a story that we'll look at in the next chapter.

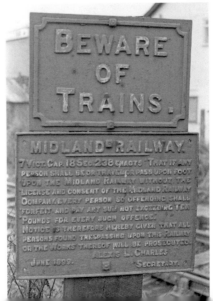

Chapter Two

UP THROUGH THE PEAK

As I said at the end of the last chapter, until I started to travel regularly to Newcastle upon Tyne from 1975 onwards, I very rarely travelled by rail north from Derby. Such excursions as we made were by car, so I knew the railways of the area from the lineside rather than from the train. But from an early age I was well aware of the great triangular junction at Ambergate.

Ambergate

In medieval times the area to the north of Derby was covered by a royal hunting forest known as the Duffield Frith. Many place names in the area reflect this history; Belper had a large area of open land known as 'The Parks', which is now recognised as part of the hunting forest; I lived on Sandbed Lane, above the Parks, which ran from Bargate to Openwoodgate ('gate' reflecting an entrance to the forest). Elsewhere in the area was Shottle Gate. Ambergate is another place name connected with the hunting forest, although the name may also refer to a toll gate on the turnpike road, opened in 1820, which now forms the

A6 Derby-Matlock road. The place itself is formed by the confluence of the rivers Amber and Derwent; it is a natural junction for routes going due north to Matlock and the Peak, and north-east towards Chesterfield. We have already encountered Ambergate in spirit in the previous chapter; Nottingham London Road station was the headquarters of the Ambergate, Nottingham & Boston & Eastern Junction Railway, which got nowhere near Ambergate. Resonant railway company titles were endemic during the Railway Mania of the 1840s, and one line that did get built was the Manchester, Buxton, Matlock & Midland Junction Railway, which ran from here into the heart of the Peak District – and which petered out at Rowsley when it ran up against the wrath of the Duke of Devonshire who refused to allow the line to be built through Chatsworth Park. The line was worked by the Midland until 1871, when it bought out the original company.

The settlement of Ambergate had no existence before the Stephensons built the North Midland

All the station buildings of the third, triangular station were in timber, and only the railway cottages and the goods shed were built of stone and survive. Here we see the original North Midland goods shed, with a loading gauge over the doorway. This building is an original Francis Thompson structure, and marks the location of the original Ambergate station.

Railway through the area, although there was a village further up the east bank of the Derwent at Toadmoor. George Stephenson encountered difficult geology in making the short Toadmoor Tunnel, and had to adopt a elliptical cross-section to allow for ground movements. Francis Thompson designed the fine station building, which was located to the north of the tunnel. When the Matlock line was opened in 1849 it connected with the Midland main line in a northerly direction only; a direct south-to-north-west connecting curve only opened in 1863, and at that point the original station building was demolished and relocated to the south of Toadmoor Tunnel, in the 'V' of the new junction. The new station building used many features and materials from the original, but was built to a new plan befitting its role as a junction station, and was considerably enlarged at the same time. It remained in use until 1876, when the new, triangular station at Ambergate was built, enabling stopping trains on the route to Chesterfield to call without obstructing the main line. From that time the old station building ceased to serve in that function, but a new use was found for it as a plans store. It continued to serve in that role until demolition in the 1960s, and I have a vague recollection of seeing it at that time.

ABOVE Just between the goods shed and the north portal of Toadmoor Tunnel there was a selection of ancillary buildings of indeterminate origin. My father Ted is seen on the right standing outside what was used as a bike shed in the 1920s – as the sign inside clearly demonstrates!

ABOVE When we visited in 1975 the only surviving timber structure from Midland times was the access stairway to platform level. The station nameboard on the one remaining platform was still, surprisingly, a BR London Midland Region enamel example. The Midland-pattern diagonal fencing has seen better days.

ABOVE This picture shows the rather fine bridge over Newbridge Road. The entrance to the second, junction station was just beyond this bridge up the road on the right. Ambergate is still known for its selection of fine masonry bridges, but this rather pleasant one with wrought-iron railings is usually overlooked.

Cromford

The Peak line wound up through the Derwent valley, paralleling the A6 and the Cromford Canal for some considerable distance. It passed a station at Whatstandwell, then shortly before Cromford station passed through the natural amphitheatre of Cromford Meadows before arriving in the station, a mixture of styles with a most ornate platform building and a station master's house that had a tendency towards the Gothic. A temporary station was opened here in 1849, as the railway company was engaged in negotiations with Richard Arkwright (son of Sir Richard, the famous local mill-owner and originator of the 'spinning jenny') over the exact location and nature of the station facilities to be provided at Cromford. Arkwright favoured a location at the south end of Cromford Meadows, nearer to the Cromford & High Peak's Sheep

Pasture Bottom and the wharf on the Cromford Canal, as being more conducive to his business interests. Matters ran out of hand as the negotiations dragged on and local residents and businessmen began to demand some sort of conclusion so that they could have confidence in the facilities to be provided. However, Arkwright's interests in the Cromford Canal continued to influence his view, and he insisted that the railway did not provide any goods facilities at the temporary station so as to safeguard his investment. Later in 1850, after local pressure continued, he relented and allowed the railway company to arrange for Cromford station to accept parcels traffic. About this time Arkwright abandoned any interest in influencing the location of the station, leaving the railway free to develop the site now generally accepted as 'Cromford station'.

LEFT The Manchester, Buxton, Matlock & Midland Junction Railway retained some vestiges of control over the line until 1871, when the Midland took full ownership and control – until then it had merely operated the trains – and within a year instructions had been given to investigate the possibilities for improving facilities at Cromford. It took a year to acquire the necessary land, the Midland having to continue the agreement originally struck with Richard Arkwright not to provide goods facilities at the station, and the contract for the new station buildings was awarded in 1874. The new building was completed a year later. The footbridge was erected by the Butterley company in 1885.

Although the station was reduced to an unstaffed halt by BR, by the 1970s Cromford had become a conservation area, and the station was included in this. The main building was acquired in 1973 by the County of Greater London South Scouts for use as dormitory space for trekking expeditions, but is now used as offices by the Arkwright Society.

ABOVE The original permanent buildings are these on the up (southbound) side. The station master's house (seen here in the background) appears to have been the first to be built, in about 1855, to the designs (it is believed) of G. H. Stokes, son-in-law to Sir Joseph Paxton, designer of the Crystal Palace but previously head gardener at the Duke of Devonshire's Chatsworth residence, to the north. Paxton had achieved national fame through his designs for the Crystal Palace in 1850, but as a director of the Midland Railway he had a certain influence on railway matters! Given that most gardeners do not become company directors, we may gather that Paxton was no ordinary individual. The ornate platform building was erected in about 1860, and served for a time as the main station building. It has since been converted to an attractive holiday cottage.

Matlock Bath

Plunging immediately into Willersley Tunnel, the line emerged in a deep cutting that gave onto Matlock Bath station, a confection in another mix of styles that were supposed to allow the traveller to draw comparisons with Switzerland.

BELOW When the line was singled the up-side platform and its ornate buildings were demolished; the separate buildings on the down side survived, though a series of awnings forming an extended canopy along the length of the platform were removed and the roofline cut back to the wall, leaving the main building looking decidedly cropped. The furthest station building was a later addition in about 1875, in a similar style to the main station building, while the station master's house was added as late as 1924 by the LMS. Matlock Bath station closed to passengers in 1967, but reopened in 1972, a year after these photographs were taken.

BOTTOM The goods facilities were to the south of the station, and appear to have been something of an afterthought. The station seems to have been intended mainly for passenger traffic, and it wasn't until 1863 that any thought was given to providing any sidings for goods traffic. Nothing happened for two years, then sidings were finally laid; a further nine years elapsed before tenders were opened for the construction of a goods shed. Although a contract was let for a shed at that time, it seems that there were second thoughts, and a further tender was opened in 1882. The shed – the large timber structure seen here – was finished early in 1883. It was joined by a pre-cast concrete animal feed store erected by the LMS at some time around the Second World War; this standard LMS structure had disappeared by the time this photograph of the goods shed was taken in 1973; it had stood to the left of the shed in this picture (i.e. to the north). The picture also shows a standard corrugated-iron LMS lamp hut on the far side of the running line. The goods shed was demolished in 1984.

Matlock

After Matlock Bath station the line plunged into High Tor No 1 Tunnel, which ran close to the rock face of the gorge through which the Derwent ran between Matlock Bath and Matlock itself. A short gap between that tunnel and High Tor No 2 Tunnel was filled in with brick arches in 1893 following repeated rock falls. After No 2 Tunnel the line crossed first the River Derwent, then the A6 at the town's southern extremity, close by the Boat Inn. It then entered Holt Lane Tunnel, to emerge from a road overbridge into Matlock station itself.

As Matlock had been the administrative centre of Derbyshire since 1956, it was sometimes necessary for us to travel there. Later, I used to go quite regularly as I had a girlfriend who lived at the top of Matlock Bank, at one time site of the world's steepest cable tramway. Derbyshire County Council's headquarters were (and still are) located in Smedley's Hydro, three-quarters of the way up Matlock Bank, and it was funny to see the reaction of councillors every time a new council got elected. Within three days or so of the first council meeting, some councillor would crop up in the local press speculating about the possibility of reinstating the tramway, even though it closed in 1927!

North of Matlock the landscape changes and the line runs through a broad valley until well beyond Bakewell. But in my time the metals stopped at Matlock, although more recently Peak Rail has restored the line between Matlock and Rowsley. The

engine shed there is long gone, although Peak Rail has recently erected a new shed on the foundations of the old. The group's long-term aim has always been to restore the railway through to Buxton, though this plan has suffered an equally long-term setback due to the demolition of the rail overbridge at Rowsley and the widening of the A6 at this point. Moreover, if Peak Rail was successful in surmounting that barrier, it would have to meet the maintenance costs of a number of tunnels, together with the great viaducts at Monsal Dale and Miller's Dale. There was some talk around the time that Virgin Trains' franchise was up for renewal of the possibility of reinstating the Matlock-Buxton-Chinley link to enable VT to use the Midland route to Manchester as an alternative route for London trains, or to allow easier access to Manchester for Virgin Cross-Country services, but nothing came of it. The study done at that time was instructed to only estimate traffic levels that would be generated by local residents, rather than take any strategic traffic levels into account…

We see first the main station building at Matlock, complete with its glazed canopy. The building, dating from 1850, was originally designed by Sir Joseph Paxton, whom we have already encountered (in spirit) at Cromford. A pleasant building in an Italianate style not seen elsewhere on the line, it was remodelled and considerably enlarged in 1888.

Facing the station across the forecourt was the station master's house, put up in 1853 as a security measure, as the goods shed had been broken into on a number of occasions. This house was also designed by Paxton. Note the BR crew bus standing in the background.

This platform view shows the range of buildings on the up side. Both buildings date from 1850; the main one, the more southerly of the two, has had the platform canopy cut back by British Rail to ease maintenance, albeit in a more sympathetic way than was done at Matlock Bath. The cutting-back reveals details of the roof brackets, which show similarities to Paxton's original station building a little further north at Rowsley (the nearest station to the Duke of Devonshire's estate at Chatsworth). Despite singling, the station still carries a number of LMR enamel signs, including one proclaiming this still to be 'Platform 1'. We are looking south here, so can see the overbridge that carries Holt Lane over the railway, with the north portal of Holt Lane Tunnel just out of sight around the bend. There is also a rather fine telegraph pole by the bridge; indeed, when these photographs were taken in 1973 the station and yard still boasted a fine array of Midland-era poles, despite the fact that they were carrying very few wires by this time.

The ruined folly of Riber Castle is prominent on the hilltop behind the town. Originally built by local entrepreneur John Smedley in 1862 as his private home, it looked over the valley onto his Hydropathic Establishment. Smedley died in 1874, but his wife continued to occupy the property until her death in 1892. It was then sold and became a boys' school until 1929, when it was offered for sale. The site was secured by the local council as a landmark, then with the coming of the Second World War the War Office took over the site but handed it on to the Ministry of Food as a storage depot; it was handed back to the council in 1948. The building gradually deteriorated until the 1960s when it became a wildlife park; this remained in business until 2000, when the owner tried, unsuccessfully, to sell it as a going concern. In 2005 plans emerged to convert the property into apartments as a means of preserving the Grade II listed structure, but these met with a deal of local opposition. Planning permission was granted in 2006, but it was conditional on the developer restoring the Castle itself. Work on that phase of the project started at the end of 2011.

ABOVE Goods facilities were quite extensive at Matlock. The first picture here shows a general view looking north from the platform; the ground frame is a poor replacement for Matlock's notable elevated signal box, which was beyond the goods shed. The frame itself is another instance of an LNWR lever frame being used in an outdoor location, as the design was quite weatherproof compared with the Midland frames. At this stage stone was still being moved by rail from the quarry out of the picture to the left. This and later pictures show a great deal of evidence of the yard's use by a local scrap metal merchant. The second picture gives a better view of the extent of the goods yard sidings; a lamp hut, a loading gauge and more telegraph poles can be seen in the distance. A grounded PW trolley and

various scrap vehicles in different states of distress litter the yard. Many of these would be considered classics today…

FACING PAGE TOP The original goods shed is a close copy of the Francis Thompson example we have already seen at Ambergate, though Thompson wasn't involved in the architecture of the original MBM&MJR line. We can also see that the yard was still used extensively by coal merchants as late as 1973.

FACING PAGE BOTTOM The coal offices and weighbridge were still occupied in 1973, but they only had another year to go, being demolished in 1974.

Dore & Totley

With the closure of the Peak line, anyone wanting to travel to Manchester from Derby either had to take a roundabout route via Uttoxeter, Stoke, Crewe and the West Coast line, or (rather shorter but still not exactly direct) they had to travel to Sheffield, then via the Hope Valley line. By the time I had to make that journey in the 1990s, it meant going all the way into Sheffield, as the station at Dore & Totley, where one could change from a Derby train to a Manchester one without going into Sheffield, was long closed to trains from Derby, and the buildings converted into a printer's office and a garden centre.

Dore & Totley station had opened in 1872, but it did not become a junction until 1893, when the Hope Valley line opened. An independent company had

obtained an Act of Parliament for this line in 1884, but rapidly ran out of money and had to approach the Midland, which was pleased to take over the project. Given the scale of the engineering required, mainly the two great tunnels at Totley and Cowburn, this was probably as well. The island platforms at Dore & Totley dated from the 1899-1905 period, when the Midland quadrupled the line from here into Sheffield and put additional platforms at all the intermediate stations.

ABOVE AND LEFT In 1973 the road side of Dore & Totley station presented a dour aspect to the intending traveller. The platform side was little better, with a handless clock; at least passengers were granted a shelter! The Hope Valley platforms seem little changed from the station's heyday, as long as you don't look too closely; the Derby line platforms are a different matter, with the up-side platform buildings boarded up. Passenger comforts seem not to have been too extensive in the first place.

In the second picture we see the Derby line curving off to the left; the chord connecting the Derby and Hope Valley lines is out of sight. Of interest are the different ventilators and roof lights for the toilet block on the island platform buildings (these appear to be of a similar design to those that survived into the 1990s at Water Orton), and the large London Midland Region station nameboard. The Hope Valley line has since been singled at this point and the island platforms demolished.

The Hope Valley line

By the time I visited in 1972 and 1973, the Hope Valley line had few station buildings remaining of much interest, though Bamford and Hathersage still retained them. Grindleford was also of interest as its booking office, separated from the platforms, served a useful purpose as a café for walkers.

ABOVE The first picture of the Hope Valley line shows the west portal of Totley Tunnel, constructed, so it tells us, in 1893. It is 6,230 yards, or 3½ miles (5.7 kilometres) long, and this photograph shows that ventilation was something of a problem on the day I visited, despite the tunnel having five ventilation shafts. A pall of diesel exhaust hangs in the tunnel mouth; apparently ventilation engineers who provided fresh air systems for recent relaying have commented that the airflow here is quite often from each end in towards the centre. To the left of the equipment cupboards can be seen a BR concrete gradient post, and behind them the tunnel nameboard, showing the length. To the right of that can be seen some cable trunking. The tunnel itself carries a plate declaring it to be bridge number 9 on this route.

RIGHT The next picture shows bridge number 10 at the Sheffield end of Grindleford station. Prominent is the rather fine lattice-post bracket signal forming the Starter signal. This is a replacement for an earlier signal, to judge by the light patch on the bridge behind it, which would have formed a sighting board for a more conventional single-post signal – and also the simple fact of this being a lattice-post signal, not a commonplace

design on the Midland or LMS! The alert reader will have also noticed that the signal is located on the wrong side of the track; this is because Grindleford station is on a sweeping left-hand curve, so the signal will have been placed in this location to allow for earliest sighting by oncoming drivers. The diamond-shaped plate on the signal indicates that it is protected by track circuiting, so Rule 55 does not apply – this is the rule requiring drivers of trains held at a signal for any length of time to contact the signal box to make certain that the signalman hasn't forgotten them. A failure to carry out this rule properly was a cause of the Hawes Junction accident on the Settle & Carlisle on Christmas Eve 1910, where a signalman did just that and caused the down Scotch Express to be incinerated. Interestingly, on the left of the picture is a telephone cabinet. Given that the Midland was slow to introduce track circuiting, even after the Board of Trade inspector recommended it in his report into the Hawes accident, this suggests that the cabinet may well date from well before the First World War.

ABOVE As late as 1973, Grindleford's freight facilities were still largely intact. The timber goods shed is a little reminiscent of that at Matlock Bath, and a local coal merchant is still using the yard and may even still be receiving coal by rail. The weighbridge is still operational, and in the picture we can see that it still sports a boot-scraper outside the door! And there are still fire buckets on the end wall of the goods shed, even if they are slowly being obscured by foliage.

BELOW Here is Grindleford signal box, an LMS structure with a steel staircase and the toilet on the veranda. There's also an LMS lamp hut and a brick-built platelayers' cabin, and the elevated cable routing mentioned earlier can be seen terminating at the box. There's also another telephone cabinet just in front of the lamp hut.

RIGHT The main station building was separate from the platforms at road level. No longer in use as a booking office, it provided (and may still provide) a welcome café for walkers, and was notorious in some quarters for the legendary rudeness of the former owner! It also boasted a little souvenir shop and information centre for the Peak District National Park. This picture gives a good idea of the structure. Note the Midland bench seat outside, another BR London Midland Region enamel sign, and the 1970s-era BR posters. The Austin A35 is noteworthy, too.

ABOVE Platform buildings were by this time rather spartan. The Manchester platform at least had this structure, though it provided passengers with no shelter; the Sheffield platform had a brick-built 'bus shelter' and little else. Of rather more interest is the rather fine Midland gas lamp, which is not only still working on gas but also lit! And at this late stage, Grindleford still boasted BR 'totem' name signs.

RIGHT At Hathersage the station building was still intact, though boarded up and disused. The platforms were comparatively short and of mainly timber construction, with ugly stone-built waiting shelters. More notably, in 1973 Hathersage still (nominally) boasted engine watering facilities – the water tower and a complete Midland water column, complete with canvas bag! The top cap is missing from the water column, and I suspect the water had been officially turned off some time before.

Seen here a year earlier, the next station, at Bamford, was in a poor state of repair, albeit mainly intact. Again, the station signage was classic BR LMR maroon, but most of the gas lamps were out of use, having been replaced by modern sodium lamps. Only those at the foot of the staircases remained intact and connected up. No one felt that the LMS tubular Starter signal needed a sighting board. The Midland diagonal station fencing, however, was mainly still in place. Again, there were the same ugly stone shelfers, and the platforms were not as well maintained as those at Grindleford.

ABOVE Hope station is seen here in 1973, looking eastwards. By this time it had been reduced to a basic calling point, and the only item of interest was the fine Midland lattice footbridge. At least on this (albeit dull) August afternoon the service was well patronised by walkers and other day-trippers.

BELOW Edale had been reduced to even more of a basic station, though it retained lay-by sidings, the necessary pointwork for trains to reverse here to work back to Sheffield, and even a loading dock!

Buxton

The Peak line itself still retained some use in the Buxton area, as that became the outer limit for commuting into Manchester. Buxton station survived as half of its former self, with only the LNWR side remaining of what was previously a rather distinguished double station.

We see here the surviving gable end of the LNWR station and, perhaps in compensation for what has been lost, a rather fine wrought-iron street lamp standard. By this time the overall roof of the LNWR station had also been demolished; it went in 1969-70 as a consequence of the ongoing cost of maintenance. Note also the fine line-up of the best the automotive industry had to offer at the time – left to right, a Ford Corsair, a Renault 4, a Sunbeam Rapier (not an original, but the badge-engineered coupé version of the Hillman Hunter), and an actual Hillman Hunter. (I owned a Hunter, once; Hillman claimed that the engine had been canted over to one side to provide more room in the engine compartment, making access for servicing easier. Why the company made this claim is open to doubt, because all the bits you needed to get at – the plugs, distributor and so on – were on the side towards which the engine was canted. In the yawning chasm on the nearside of the car was the carburettor and air filter and that was all. To make matters worse, the

windscreen washer bottle was actually a bag, hung off the battery securing plate; if you had to do any work on the plugs and points, in leaning over the offside wing of the car your right elbow was inevitably squeezing this bag in the manner of someone playing the bagpipes. After 10 minutes you wondered why you had a wet arm – because you'd inevitably squeezed a quantity of the washer water out through the bag's vent hole…)

Buxton was served by both the Midland and the LNWR. The Duke of Devonshire, working through Sir Joseph Paxton, arranged matters so that both companies cooperated over the design of their stations at Buxton, and both stations boasted an ornate glazed end wall befitting their central location. The stations were parallel to each other and both had overall roofs. However, the Midland station was an early victim of the closure of the Peak line, the overall roof and end wall being demolished in 1964. It finally closed in 1967; there was a brief attempt by the Peak Railway Society to bring railway activity back to the site in the 1980s with the establishment of the 'Buxton Steam Centre', but intransigence by British Rail, in not countenancing any idea of Peak Rail using the Great Rocks Dale line, resulted in the closure of this attraction to concentrate activities on the southern headquarters of the group's project at Darley Dale. The Midland station site finally disappeared under a bypass later in the decade.

This picture shows the surviving LNWR station building; the Midland one, which faced it across the station access road, was identical. Neither were exceptional gems of architecture, as this picture shows. So let's look at the cars again, instead. There's an early BMW 1600, dating from the time before the Bavarian product became an object of desire, and an Austin 1800, the infamous 'Land Crab', a huge car with a wheel at each corner, a transverse engine and gas-filled suspension. And as ugly as a box of frogs. I don't think I've ever seen one of these restored as a 'classic' – I suspect that even if you could find an enthusiast for one, they'd have found re-pressurising the suspension beyond them. And probably a good thing, too. In the background is a Morris Minor with a 'G' registration – yes, BMC was still turning these out in 1969! – and behind it a Wolseley 1500, a chubby little four-door saloon with the style, performance and handling of a Dralon-covered settee.

ABOVE Without referring to historic photographs, it was difficult to get any idea as to the layout at Buxton Midland with the track gone and grass growing all over the site. As a late-comer, the Midland station was rather shoehorned onto a very cramped site; the LNWR lines dominated the station layout. Buxton No 2 signal box is on the embankment originally built for the Ashbourne line, but which now serves the rump of the Midland route for quarry traffic, using the chord put in to the one-time Buxton East Junction. It controlled access to the stump of the former Midland route down to Blackwell and into Great Rocks Dale for the quarry traffic. It is a typical LNWR-pattern box, and some idea of the complexity of the layout at Buxton can be judged by its size and the knowledge that it was the second such box on the LNWR side of the station. The Midland side also boasted two boxes, Buxton Station and Buxton East Junction. The signal in the background is on the chord connecting the Ashbourne line to the northern end of the station layout.

BELOW These huts on the Midland side were the survivors of quite a 'colony' of assorted ad hoc structures in this area; photographic evidence for them can be found dating back to 1914, though the example on the right, which seems to use a lot of Midland signal box components, could well be older. The left-hand hut bears the title 'Signal Dept.' and, to judge by the insulators on the gable, had a telephone run into it, so it may well have been the home of the signalling linesman for Buxton Midland.

It's now easy to forget that, back in the days before digital cameras, photography was limited by how many films you had with you and how many exposures you had left on your last roll! I recollect finding myself on the horns of a dilemma over what else to photograph at Buxton when I was down to my last two frames, this being a late summer Sunday evening with no likelihood of finding a shop open that might sell film, and I finally used my last frame to capture an image of an old LMS coach being used as a snowplough riding van. Even in August a snowplough was an essential part of Buxton's railway equipment; in my youth, the start of a Derbyshire winter was often a radio announcement that Buxton was cut off by snow! I never went back to Buxton to take pictures, so anyone wanting views of the platform side of the LNWR station will have to look elsewhere.

Hayfield and New Mills

The railway back into Manchester became increasingly complex, with the LNWR line to Buxton having quite extensive commuter traffic. So it was that places like New Mills could still, in the early 1970s, boast two stations, with Newtown (a rather simple affair) serving the LNWR line, while Central, on the Midland line to Marple, Romiley, Hyde and Guide Bridge, suddenly found itself on the main route between Sheffield and Manchester with the closure of Manchester Central in favour of putting all traffic into Piccadilly. New Mills Central was also the junction for the branch to Hayfield (later to achieve some fame as the location for the surreal BBC television comedy show The League of Gentlemen, where it portrayed the fictional town of Royston Vasey), and a stump of this remained when I visited in the early 1970s. No such luck for the branch itself, though; the service ceased on 5 January 1970, and when I visited two years or so later the line had been lifted not long before, and the remaining structures were coming to the attention of the local youth with too much time on their hands.

ABOVE The station is seen here with gas lamp-posts and even a point lever (visible in front of the gable end of the station building extension) visible. The Midland diagonal-pattern fencing has suffered, though, and indeed much of it appears to have been replaced before closure. The station forecourt is still being used as a bus stop at this time, with a SELNEC Alexander-bodied bus waiting for business and a timetable board visible in front of the asbestos shed to the left of the picture. (Without being able to make out a fleet or registration number, it's difficult to say whether the bus is a Daimler Fleetline or a Leyland Atlantean.)

BELOW The Midland signal box at Hayfield is a study in blackened timber, ash and carbonisation. It had probably only been set on fire a day or so beforehand; smoke can still be seen rising from the ashes. More to the point, it's perhaps remarkable that the lever frame and point rodding were still in situ, more than two years after closure. There is another lamp-post still in place on the right of the crossing gates, and the picture also shows the arrangement of the cabling run from the terminal telegraph pole into the box.

New Mills Newtown, seen here looking south towards Buxton, was a simple, undistinguished station, but still with a goodly complement of gas lamps and BR totem signs. The LNWR line opened in 1857 as the Stockport, Disley and Whaley Bridge Railway, and it was extended to Buxton in 1864. In this picture a BR Class 104 DMU departs for Buxton. The DMU's white roof is noteworthy, as are the 1972 fashions! Gordon Biddle, in his compendious gazeteer on railway architecture, devotes serious attention to this footbridge, and then adds that there's a similar one at Whaley Bridge, a few miles away on the same line; but of the more architecturally notable buildings at New Mills Central on the Midland line, he ays nothing. Well, we can put that right....

This is New Mills Central, looking west towards Marple – a neat station, with a Midland-pattern bench seat visible on the down platform, and (just visible below the main station canopy) a set of mounting steps to compensate for a comparatively low platform here. It may seem odd that a Midland station is called 'Central', but this is a reminder of some complex 19th century railway politics. This line started out as the independent Marple, New Mills and Hayfield Junction Railway, which lasted a whole four days after its opening on 1st July 1865 before being absorbed by the Manchester, Sheffield & Lincolnshire - later the Great Central - though the Marple company had a longer existence as another 'brass plaque' operation. Almost from the start, the MSLR made an agreement with the Midland for joint running over this line, to give the Midland access to Manchester and to thwart the ambitions of the LNWR in the area. This was formalised in 1869 with the incorporation of the Sheffield & Midland Joint Committee.

Here we see Central's rather distinguished Jacobean-style station buildings, which date from the opening of the line in 1865. Note the little trefoil pinnacle on the gable end nearest the camera; another may be made out on the gable of the dormer window. This device was the trademark of the unknown architect (or perhaps the mason) of all the stations on the Marple line, and can be seen on other buildings in the area. We can also see the location of the signal box controlling the junction for the Hayfield branch and the down side lay-by siding to the west of the station.

Next is a view of the box itself, from a slightly unusual viewpoint. We get an excellent view of the run-out from the box, and the plank walkway over the rodding run to the ground signal. The coal bunker, cable conduit and toilet hut are also nicely visible, as indeed are the box's foundations, something not often seen. There is a lamp illuminating the stairs, and someone has nailed a small tray to the handrail on the veranda outside the door, just the right size for two mugs of tea. There's a standard LMS lamp hut on the right of the picture. The other point of interest is that the lever frame here is at the back of the box, not the front. This may well have been done so as to allow the signalman easier access to the front of the box to observe passing trains, given the restricted view along the line at this point; but locating the frame at the back of the box would make access to the interlocking difficult, as on Midland frames this was located behind the levers and above floor level.

Woodhead

Of course, at that time there was another route between Manchester and Sheffield – the Great Central line via Woodhead. This route had ceased to take passenger traffic between the two cities in 1970, but it was still ostensibly open for freight, and there was suburban traffic at each end.

Woodhead itself was a spectacular location. The accompanying photographs, taken in 1977, show the line on a Sunday when there was no freight running. Sadly, I never got to see any trains running on the Woodhead route, though I did manage to photograph some locomotives standing at one of the depots near Sheffield from a moving train on a Sunday engineering diversion. The line closed in 1981 and the rails were lifted, after a number of years of decline in freight traffic and in the face of increasing costs

of maintaining or renewing the by now non-standard 1,500V DC traction equipment. The Woodhead route retains a grip on the railway enthusiast's imagination, and a number of schemes have been proposed in the years since closure to bring it back into use. It was most recently mentioned in connection with the new rail infrastructure project for Manchester known as the Northern Hub, when the MP for Penistone and Stocksbridge, Angela C. Smith, raised the question of reinstating the line. She had previously been MP for Sheffield Hillsborough from 2005, and had campaigned for reinstatement during that Parliament. Unfortunately, without a renaissance of rail freight across the Pennines, such a prospect seems unlikely, given that the Hope Valley line has sufficient capacity for all foreseeable growth in passenger rail traffic.

RIGHT The first picture shows a general view of the station – all BR buildings from the late 1950s/early 1960s, built in stone. This picture also shows the 'new' Woodhead Tunnel portal. This tunnel, sometimes referred to as Woodhead 3, was built in 1953 for the completion of the line's electrification, as the earlier two single-track bores (whose portals are just out of view to the left of the main running lines) were very narrow and did not possess sufficient space for the overhead equipment. Woodhead 3 had the trans-Pennine power line installed in it in 2008 as the cable in Woodhead 1 was becoming life-expired. Woodhead 2 has suffered rock falls and is no longer passable.

LEFT The second photograph shows the dramatic view looking west down the Longendale valley in fairly typical Pennine weather, taken from just above the tunnel portal. The arrangements for the power cables running into Woodhead 1 and 2 tunnels are prominent.

Glossop and Dinting

From Manchester, suburban electrics ran out to Glossop, past the rather nice preservation centre at Dinting, located on a spectacular plateau at the top of a steep hill with a fine view of Dinting viaduct.

The Dinting Railway Centre was one of the early preservation sites that housed former main-line engines. The Bahamas Locomotive Society obtained the site in 1968, and spent 20 years there, erecting a rather fine steel museum building before the lease expired in 1988. The history of what happened to the museum is complex and mired in legalese, but the upshot was that BR either asked too much for renewal of the lease, or made a mess out of the renewal process (or both), and the backers of the preservation group had little choice but to walk away. Much of the physical equipment went to the East Lancashire Railway, while the Bahamas Locomotive Society itself moved to Ingrow on the Keighley & Worth Valley Railway. Other locomotives based at Dinting went to other owners and other lives. The site itself was left to languish, being an odd shape, in a particularly wild location, with no planning permission and standing outside the Glossop development zone. There were also some concerns over it being contaminated land, as much of the site was made up with ash and other tailings from Gorton Works (or so it was said). The site came up for sale in September 2010, and a trust went to auction armed with a war chest of some £150,000, but the fall of bidding favoured a developer who narrowly beat the preservationists to it. The railway centre museum building erected by the preservationists has now disappeared, while the original MSLR shed is derelict.

ABOVE Meanwhile, Greater Manchester PTE buses wait for custom, an inconvenient distance away from the station entrance. The leading vehicle is KJA 294G, a former North Western Bristol RESL with a Marshall body. There is an interesting timber coal merchant's office by the goods yard entrance gates and some more period cars, including a rather fine-looking Riley 4/72.

LEFT AND ABOVE Glossop station frontage is seen here, with another fine collection of 1970s motoring machinery. Note that the illuminated light fittings still call this 'Glossop Central', not that there was any other station with which it could be confused – at least, not since 1845 when this branch was opened and the former Glossop station, a mile away, was renamed Dinting! This station was at the end of a short branch, built in 1844 at the personal expense of the Duke of Norfolk – hence the rather haughty lion surmounting the station front entrance! The building dates from 1848.

BELOW AND RIGHT The outside of the ticket office has been decorated in time for the Silver Jubilee. The ticket window's surround is notable. The clock is by Arnold & Lewis of Manchester and carries the serial number 603. The post box on the left of the picture – also seen in close-up in the second photo – is of Victorian origin, of a style that started to appear from 1881.

ABOVE The platform view shows the extent to which the layout at Glossop had been rationalised. The goods sheds have since been incorporated into a Co-op supermarket, and the disused bay platform to the left has been brought back into use, replacing the running line shown here, which has been incorporated into the supermarket.

Dinting station occupied two sides of a triangle; it was a bleak and windswept location and the station buildings emphasised that air. The main station buildings seen here were on the up side of the main line. The signal box appears to have had reinforcing rods put through from side to side and front to back; note that the entrance is at the rear and there is a substantial landing at the top of the steps. There is also some good detail of the run-out from the box passing underneath the platform. Note the rather fine gas lamp-post to the right of the box with a BR totem nameboard still surviving.

Suburban services on the remains of the Great Central at this time were in the hands of these 1950 units, built to an LNER design but later known by British Rail as Class 506. This three-car set has Motor Brake 2nd No M59401M leading. It is seen here joining the main line from the Glossop branch, heading for Manchester. The Dinting down-side station building is visible in the background. Most suburban services traversed the Glossop branch; only a handful of contra-peak services during the morning and evening avoided the branch, shaving some 8 minutes off their 'empty' journey to get them back into position to pick up more commuters. This picture was taken 'over the fence' from the Dinting Railway Centre; the driver seems a bit surprised that anyone should be pointing a camera at *his* train!

Penistone

On the far side of the Pennines, stopping trains ran from Doncaster via Barnsley to Huddersfield through the junction station of Penistone, a name now reviled by Internet obscenity filters everywhere. Although the GC trans-Pennine service had long ceased, the Manchester platforms were intact.

The station buildings were solid and unremarkable; these 1977 pictures show that the station was fairly unchanged despite the absence of Manchester services since 1970. There were still some vestiges of the busy railway life, in the form of notices (including an original Manchester, Sheffield & Lincolnshire Railway fire hydrant sign) and a fine station clock, which was substantially intact when photographed – I hope it survived!

ABOVE The signal box was located back towards Sheffield, and was impressively elevated.

BELOW Meanwhile, on the Barnsley platforms, accommodation was rather more spartan, with only minimal canopies for passenger shelter on the main platform and none whatsoever on the island platform, just a basic waiting shelter. A Barnsley service is in the hands of a two-car DMU – not a well-patronised service on this wet Sunday. Note that the catenary ends at the gantry visible here.

Sheffield Midland

Coming back almost full circle, we are now at Sheffield Midland – not in a strict railway sense, as of course GC line trains went into Victoria, but that was closed by the time I knew Sheffield. This station had low buildings in undressed stone, and an open aspect to the railway-side arrangements that made it quite pleasant to frequent. I once came down to Sheffield from Leeds in a 'Pacer' four-wheeled railcar, which was possibly one of the most uncomfortable railway journeys I ever made.

Sheffield was not originally on the Midland main line between Derby and Leeds; when George Stephenson was setting out the route of the North Midland Railway, he had looked at the terrain and decided that Sheffield was best served by a branch from Masborough. This was done despite some very high-level interventions (including from George Hudson himself) to persuade Stephenson to put Sheffield on the NMR direct line, but Stephenson was firmly wedded to the idea of the route having a ruling gradient of no more than 1 in 130, and if that meant bypassing some major towns on the way, so be it. Barnsley and Wakefield shared Sheffield's fate of being consigned to a branch line from the North Midland.

In the following 25 years, numerous railways were built that connected Sheffield ever more into a regional network of lines in South Yorkshire and running east-west across the country. But schemes to link the town directly with Chesterfield always seemed to come to nought for one reason or another, and the ironmasters and tradesmen of Sheffield felt that the trade of the town suffered from not having a direct connection to the south. So in 1863 the citizens of Sheffield pressed for a line of their own to provide a more direct connection to Chesterfield and the south. The Midland board took note of the pressure, and quickly proposed such a line. Surveys were made, plans were drawn up, and everyone was content. But in secret, various local worthies and the Corporation of the City of Sheffield were working behind the scenes, and in August 1863 the existence of a separate proposal was suddenly unveiled.

Sheffield Midland station was designed by Charles Trubshaw, the company's in-house architect, and was built over the River Sheaf. It was the largest station on the Midland system after St Pancras. Here we see the 1905 frontage; the 300-foot-long covered taxi rank was incorporated into the station concourse in 2002. Trubshaw based his design on the one he had used at Leicester in 1892, although with this station being at almost the lowest part of the valley of the River Sheaf, and lacking any sort of tower, the overall impression is of a long, flat building, lacking the visual impact of other Midland stations of comparable size and importance. It attracted a degree of local criticism for this very reason!

ABOVE This picture shows the railway side of the station. The main island structures – now Platforms 2 to 5 – formed the original 1870 station building. The 1905 rebuilding also placed overall canopies over Platforms 1 and 2, and Platforms 5 to 8. These were damaged beyond economic repair during the Second World War and the awnings seen in these pictures were installed in 1956. The spacious nature of Sheffield Midland can be appreciated – the main platform is 700 feet long.

LEFT The principal entrance to the concourse is seen here: above the W. H. Smith bookstall can be seen the footbridge, and fine ironwork is visible throughout.

A nice period piece is this entrance to the refreshment room on Platform 1, with fine gilded letters above the door.

The original intention was to have a 'Plan B' in case the Midland either declined to build a direct line to connect Sheffield to the south, or to apply pressure on the company to keep its interest going. But in the process, someone seems to have become rather carried away. The proposed Sheffield, Chesterfield & Staffordshire Railway would not only connect Sheffield to the Midland and the MSLR, but would also extend south-westwards through the Peak District to join the North Staffordshire and London & North Western railways at Ashbourne; further, its Act of Parliament demanded the withdrawal of the Midland's own scheme and its replacement with the Midland seeking running powers over the Sheffield company's line. The latter company was also to have running powers over all of the Midland system, and it was also proposed to change the point of junction with the Manchester, Sheffield & Lincolnshire Railway to Chesterfield, whereby the Sheffield company would have running powers to Chesterfield and onto the MSLR.

But some investigation by the Midland's solicitors established that the various shareholders and promoters of the Sheffield railway had not put up the initial deposit for the Bill, but had financed it via a loan, something not legal, and when the Parliamentary Bill for the Sheffield scheme was moved, the Midland called the other company's bluff. At the Committee stage, the Sheffield scheme was rejected after some adroit questioning by the Midland's counsel as well as objections from the MSLR and the North Staffordshire (which were discouraged by the attitude of the Sheffield company towards the Midland and could see themselves being treated similarly). The Sheffield line's Bill fell and the Midland Railway Bill for the line between Sheffield and Chesterfield was passed. The promoters of the Sheffield railway attempted a rearguard action in the House of Lords, hoping to have the Midland Bill overturned there so that they could come back to Parliament with a rehash of their own scheme, but wiser councils prevailed and the Midland's Bill finally became law. The direct line from Chesterfield to Sheffield opened without any ceremony on 2 February 1870; one suspects that after all the manoeuvring, the Midland was determined to deny Sheffield any recognition or admit that a new railway in Sheffield was anything to be officially marked.

Sheffield was one of the last places where I ever saw additional carriages attached to a passenger train. Travelling down from Newcastle in the late 1970s, you approached Sheffield Midland through a tunnel, and as the train slowed to enter the station you passed one or two coaches with passengers sitting in them,

attached to an 08 shunter and standing on a headshunt inside the tunnel itself. Once our train had come to a halt, there was a delay while the 08 propelled these coaches out of the tunnel and attached them to the rear of our train to continue south. There is some evidence to suggest that these may have been part of a Hull-Brighton service, which implies that they may have been detached again at Birmingham New Street! (Certainly, in the days of the famous 'Pines Express' from Manchester to Bournemouth over the Somerset & Dorset, two coaches from Sheffield were regularly attached at Birmingham during the 1950s, and detaching and reattaching coaches had been a feature of passenger workings at Sheffield since Midland times. Even once the direct line had opened to Chesterfield, some direct London-Leeds services had slip coaches for Sheffield, which were detached at Masborough.) Of course, once the HSTs were introduced on the South West/North East route in the early 1980s, this practice ceased forever. But in any case, when I saw it this was even then probably one of the last vestiges of pre-Nationalisation railway timetabling and a remnant of a time when the Midland line ran through the Peak District.

Here we see the station's northern approach, with the tunnels under 'The Park' and the Park Hill flats prominent on the skyline. The River Sheaf flows directly beneath the station in a culvert; the water tower appears to pump water directly up from the river, to judge by the substantial rising pipe, presumably for toilet flushing or train washing purposes. There is a PW gang working immediately in front of the tunnels; the high-visibility jacket is in use here (if only by the lookout man!). It's worth remembering that health and safety is an essential part of the railway scene, so we should not be surprised at the railways being early adopters of what is now a common feature of our streets and building sites.

FACING PAGE Sheffield Midland in 1975 had something that rather took me by surprise – a gaggle of early telephone boxes. They were known by the GPO as 'type K1', and went into production in 1923, predating the more familiar classic series designed by Sir Giles Gilbert Scott. They were quite rare by the 1970s. These three pictures show a bank of three 'K1s' on the main concourse and two separate examples on other platforms. They had mainly been repainted into British Telecom's corporate black and yellow, rather disguising their age (their internal equipment had long since been modernised), but the one in the second picture was in a dark grey, as I recollect. The bank of three have illuminated 'Telephone' signs more commonly associated with the Gilbert Scott kiosks (well, two of them do), but the one on the left has contemporary 'Public Telephone' transfer lettering on the door glass – a very rare survival! And the one in the third view still has its original painted signs on the roof. I wonder if any of these were saved for posterity?

ABOVE At the bays at the Rotherham end of the station a selection of BRUTEs (BR Universal Trolley Equipment) await another consignment of parcels.

Chapter Three

GO WEST, YOUNG MAN

In 1972 my sister and her husband moved from Slough to Telford, the New Town in Shropshire. Until this time Shropshire had been something that we had driven through on our way to holidays in North Wales, but now we had the opportunity to stop and look a bit more closely. Funnily enough, that was something we had rarely done on our cross-country drive, and the other thing is that driving cross-country meant that one tended to come across individual stations rather than follow a particular line, recording the stations along the route.

Whitchurch

So that is how we came to photograph Whitchurch. The station is on the Shrewsbury & Crewe Railway, built by the LNWR and opened in 1858. Once a junction for lines to Chester and Oswestry, by the time we visited in 1973 these services had gone. The station presented a sombre appearance, being constructed in blue engineering brick throughout, but the main feature that stopped me in my tracks when I first stepped onto the platform was a fully intact LNWR water tower!

The station is still open, but the buildings have now been demolished. Only the footbridge, signal box (locked out of use) and the suspension footbridge now remain.

THIS PAGE What became obvious as we went around was that many of the station's steam-age accoutrements were generally intact. There was a water crane (complete with 'fire devil'), a water tower that had been associated with the engine shed, and a turntable – although these were no longer connected to the railway at all.

The locomotive shed started out as a two-road affair that opened in 1872. In 1883 it was replaced by a new four-road shed; this closed in 1957 with the closure of the direct line to Chester via Waverton, and although it was used for wagon repairs for a while (it was still in use in 1960) it had long gone by the time we saw the site.

LEFT There is a good deal of period interest in this general view, looking towards Shrewsbury. There is still an LMR maroon 'Way Out' sign and a vintage 'Car Stop' marker sign on the platform. The footbridge retains its ornate brackets (these were removed in the station rationalisation) and smoke shields over the running lines, though it is no longer roofed. With the demolition of the main station buildings, which included the staircase to the footbridge, a modern steel substitute had to be provided. But at this stage the fine platform canopy with its ornate supports remains, as do LNWR-period platform benches, a working clock and a luggage trolley. Closer inspection shows that this is actually Platform 2, Platform 1 being a bay at the north end of the platform.

LEFT AND BELOW The first of these two pictures shows the substantial platform buildings, while the second shows a general view looking north. The bay platform can be seen on the right, long disused (if you look closely, you'll see that one of the lamp-posts has been relocated to the trackbed!). It once sported an overall roof.

LEFT The next picture shows the signal box, a conventional LNWR structure. Note the external toilet hut with its own veranda, the ground signal and the signal guy post on the right; the latter guys the substantial double bracket signal seen in the general view (though mainly concealed by the gas lamp). The goods facilities at Whitchurch were concealed behind substantial brick walls.

The curve in the line at this point and the way that the structures obscured drivers' sight lines dictated that tall signal posts were used, together with co-acting arms; the latter were used when such a tall signal was provided, so that there was a repeater arm at the driver's normal eye level when his engine stood at the signal itself. Interestingly, this is a lattice-post signal – not a common LNWR feature – and the top stage is placed well below the upper arm, as someone seems to have decided it was better to have easy access to the guy wire attachment points – which after all might get checked once a year at best – than to make it easy to attend to the upper signal lamp, which in the days before electric lights would have needed refilling with oil on a weekly, if not daily, basis! It was necessary, for stability, to guy tall signals like these; even then, Ted often commented that climbing one of them at night, in a high wind, to seek out a fault with a signal detector could often be a daunting task! One of the guy posts can be seen on the left, a short square-section post of LNWR origin with a little pyramidal cap on it.

We also see to the left of the main signal post a smaller LMS tubular signal with a dwarf arm. It can't have been for the bay platform – that's been out of use so long that an equipment cupboard has been built on the trackbed – but it is more likely to have been provided in the place of a bracket signal to control entry to the goods yard. Notice also the bracket signal on the opposite line, now shorn of one arm as the far platform face of the island platform (Platform 4) is no longer in use.

In the background can be seen perhaps the most remarkable thing about Whitchurch – the rather astonishing 120-foot-span suspension footbridge, installed because the range

of sidings at this point left no space for the supports of a conventional bridge. It is Grade II listed, and English Heritage dates it to around 1872; Gordon Biddle speculates that this may well be unique on a British railway.

Notice also the couple of platform trolleys dumped off the end of the platform, and the assorted timbers that may well have been the remains of the bay platform overall roof.

ABOVE AND RIGHT We found Whitchurch notable for its collection of period detail. Apart from the watering facilities (and their remarkable state of preservation despite it being five years since the end of all steam on BR), there were gas lamps, an LNWR trespass notice (there appears to be no reason why the script appears as black on white instead of the other way round – either could be encountered), an LNWR bridge number plate, and an electric 'line occupied' signal repeater, found on the wall of the island platform building by Platform 4.

BELOW And finally, Ted plays the role of a passenger in this picture of the head of the footbridge stairs on the main station building.

Oakengates

When my sister moved there, there was no railway station called 'Telford'. Until Telford Central opened in 1986 the New Town was served by two pre-existing stations, Oakengates and Wellington. (There was also a short-lived halt, New Hadley, between the two, which was closed when the new Central station opened.)

The Shrewsbury & Birmingham Railway opened to Oakengates in 1849, and the station there was designed by the company's architect, Edward Banks. Since 1999 the building, somewhat altered and with some parts demolished, has served as a dentist's surgery.

TOP, ABOVE AND LEFT In the first picture Oakengates station is seen from the road entrance; only the central block of this building now survives unaltered. The next picture shows the stable block by the station entrance, with an iron foundry behind. There was also a cement silo on site, which was still sending out Presflo traffic in 1973.

RIGHT The platform side view shows the 1950s covered ramp down into the booking office, the platforms having been raised since the station opened. There are two platform barrows, and period Inter-City posters on the far wall; other attractions being advertised are the Severn Valley Railway (at that time running from Bridgnorth to Hampton Loade only) and a concert by the Shrewsbury Orchestral Society at the town's Music Hall. The station retains its London Midland Region maroon nameboard.

Of the platform trolleys, the barrow is definitely a GWR product, but the rather impressive large barrow has defied my efforts at identification thus far. Oakengates had the rather nice feature of a barrow path laid in the down platform ramp with blue engineering brick.

Wellington

The next full station along the line towards Shrewsbury was Wellington. Also opened in 1849, this station underwent far more development in its life, serving as a junction station for the LNWR line to Stafford and the GWR lines north to Nantwich and south to Coalbrookdale and Buildwas.

Wellington had a rather striking entrance. Note the ancient Ford Zodiac parked outside; back in the 1970s, a ten-year-old car was something of a rarity, as cars rotted faster and the MOT test took many older cars off the road fairly quickly. The second picture shows a GWR trespass warning notice that was located on the wall outside the station among the advertising posters. Forty shillings (£2.00) was not a lot as a fine, even then – the penalty today (2012) can be up to £1,000.

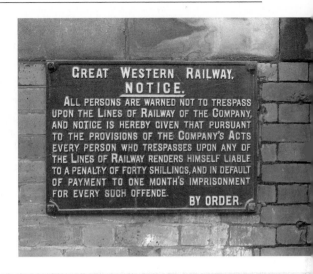

RIGHT This is a panoramic view of the station looking back towards Wolverhampton. Perhaps the most remarkable thing is the amount of parcels traffic that the station is dealing with – parcels of all shapes and sizes, including something that looks like a carpet. Back in the 1970s there were very few independent parcel courier firms, and most packages that were too big for the post went via rail or via the nationalised road equivalent, British Road Services (BRS Parcels).

LEFT AND OPPOSITE The first of these two pictures shows the main platform at Wellington (Platform 2), with fine wrought-iron canopy supports and two GWR platform benches. There is a Post Office 'K1'-type telephone kiosk on the platform, seen more closely in the second view.

LEFT At the Wolverhampton end of the station was Wellington No 2 signal box, which was a GWR 1940s construction. Off the picture to the right is the bay platform for Coalbrookdale and Buildwas services.

RIGHT This picture shows one of the older Wellington signal boxes, still in use at this time to control the section between the station and the goods yard.

RIGHT The rather fine station clock has been tastefully updated to give 24-hour-clock times.

From the roadside the entrance to the goods yard was guarded by what was one of the most ornate weighbridge huts I've ever seen, and a fine pair of GWR signs, one a standard trespass notice and the other an interesting local 'special'.

The goods yard at Wellington – 'Wellington Town Goods Depot' as it says on the side of the goods shed – was a few hundred yards beyond the station in the Shrewsbury direction. The goods shed office has seen better days; some of the equipment cupboards on its walls are getting hacked about, and there is rubbish where the siding through the shed should emerge. Guttering and downpipes are also damaged – note the considerable watermark where the downpipe should be. There is a telegraph pole, suggesting that the goods office at least had a telephone line. The goods shed itself has a lot of tie-bars and strengthening plates – there would be a lot of old mine workings in this area. The two windows over the rail door are later additions, as the remains of a painted sign saying 'Great Western Railway' can be seen between them. The fencing alongside the line has gates at regular intervals, showing it to have seen use as a cattle dock at some point (and certainly in 1956 the station could still accept livestock traffic), but now it is in use as a coal merchant's depot. We forget how recently it has been that central heating became the norm for most domestic properties; in 1975 there is still a considerable coal trade, as can be seen by the large pile of coal and the two Bedford TKs – especially the front one with a ludicrously large load of coal sacks that would certainly fall foul of modern health and safety considerations – and rightly so!

Moving the camera to the right, the down yard has a good collection of wagons in it, mainly for coal traffic but also a lot of vans, a tube wagon and one of the new twin tracklaying cranes with a riding van, not to mention a fine array of yard lamps. Just over the top of the tube wagon can be seen part of the yard crane. Meanwhile, the up yard has more vans, a partly unloaded rake of rail-carrying wagons, a substantial loading dock for the adjoining factory, and more yard lamps.

The first picture shows the road side of the goods shed, and a fine and substantial building it is, with all manner of additions, steps, lights and general kipple surrounding it. More coal merchants' lorries are parked up here.

The next picture (facing page) shows the yard hand crane, with its hook neatly tied up so as to avoid accidents with the hook weight – whether accidental accidents or not! According to the 1904 Railway Clearing House handbook, Wellington possessed crane power of 10 tons, but by 1956 this had been reduced to 3 tons – the crane seen here.

Our final picture of Wellington shows a marvellous corrugated-iron coal merchant's office, complete with a set of scales, his lorry and a diesel pump, marked 'Not for resale'.

Shrewsbury

And so to journey's end – Shrewsbury. The station building was designed by T. M. Penson for the Shrewsbury & Birmingham and Shropshire Union railways and opened in 1848; the LNWR wanted to use this station also, but was prevented from entering it with the Shrewsbury & Crewe Railway when its line was authorised by Parliament in 1853 because their Lordships wanted to force the LNWR to make a better access to the town, this main station being away from the centre of the old town at the time it was built. Instead, the LNWR's line had to terminate in a field almost a mile from the town until negotiations exhausted any other possibility of making a better entry to Shrewsbury (mere geography not being a matter that Parliament concerned itself with!), and it was three years before the final mile was authorised. The LNWR opened its Crewe line in 1858, and Shrewsbury became a joint station with the GWR. At the time the accompanying photographs were taken in 1975, this was manifested in a mixture of LNWR, LMS and GWR signals, although the signal boxes were all built on the LNWR pattern. Other fixtures and fittings showed an interesting mixture of the two companies' styles.

BELOW AND TOP RIGHT The frontage of Shrewsbury station was specifically designed to match the adjacent Shrewsbury School, given that the geography of Shrewsbury severely limited the railway as to where a major station could be sited. Interestingly, the station as opened was only a two-storey building, and the gabled extension on the left of the first picture was added in 1855 by Penson. In 1903, the then chief engineer for the LNWR and GWR Joint Committee, R. E. Johnston, underpinned the existing building, excavated the forecourt and put a new third storey in, underneath the existing building!

We should also take the time to look at a couple of interesting details in the forecourt; the rare 'K4' telephone kiosk and automatic post office, and the LMS/GWR Joint 'Private Road' notice, with a 1930s traffic sign, studded with brilliants, below it. The 'K4' kiosk was designed in 1925 as an expansion of Sir Giles Gilbert Scott's iconic 'K2' kiosk. It went into production in 1930, but proved unsatisfactory; the rolls of stamps in the vending machines tended to gum up, while the clunk of the vending machines disturbed people making telephone calls. The redesign to incorporate the post box and vending machines rendered the whole kiosk out of proportion when compared with the earlier 'K2'; only 50 were made, and the last was installed in 1935.

RIGHT This is the rear of the main 1849 station building, and it is clearly a two-storey building on the platform side. The long platform here – Platform 3 – was not in use for passenger traffic at all, but dealt with parcels traffic, hence the lack of any signage whatsoever, not even a station name. The platform is well stocked with BRUTEs, the standard 1970s BR parcels trolley. 'BRUTE' was short for British Rail Universal Trolley Equipment – someone must have felt very pleased with themselves for thinking up that acronym!

LEFT Looking towards Crewe, this is Crewe Junction and its signal box, which is standard LNWR, though its rear retaining wall extends well below rail level. The gantry, however, is pure GWR, with lower-quadrant arms and route indicators. To the left of the box, a tank wagon parked in a siding can just be made out. The Crewe lines diverge sharply to the right.

ABOVE Shrewsbury is now perhaps best known for Severn Bridge Junction signal box, which, with its 180 levers, is now reputed to be the largest working mechanical signal box in the world. A gigantic version of the standard LNWR pattern box, it was built in 1903 and controls the southern approaches to Shrewsbury from both the Wolverhampton and Hereford directions. It has an internal staircase, and is a Listed structure.

BELOW Visible from Platform 7 is the connection into the goods yard, which had not long been taken up to judge by the spare sleepers dumped in the ballast. Also seen is the rear of another GWR signal with a big, old timber post and a shunting signal. Next to it appears to be the remains of a gas lamp, and next to that is a rather well-worn loading gauge. There is a loading dock on the left – note the steps behind the signal – and because the bridge under Howard Street is on a skew the resulting passage was obviously considered long enough to require a platelayers' refuge.

This view of the station looking back from the Wolverhampton end shows all seven platforms. From left to right, Platforms 1 and 2 are bays where a coach is standing; Platform 3, then used for parcels only, is marked by the pre-cast concrete platform units; the platform in the middle of the picture has Platform 4 as the far face and Platform 5 facing; the photograph is taken from the ramp at the end of Platform 6; and Platform 7 is beyond that. Platforms 5 and 6 form another bay. The concrete platform extension to Platform 3 was part of the remodelling works in 1962 to relay some of the junctions, install new connections and generally ease working arrangements at that end of the station. And of the coach in the Platform 1 bay, I'll venture that this is something rather special; it is of LNWR design, it is non-corridor and it looks like 50-foot stock.

Beyond that, I've drawn a blank. In the 1880s and 1890s the LNWR produced coaches like this in a bewildering combination of compartments, half-compartments, lavatories and luggage compartments, and I've not been able to match this with any identifiable plans in my possession. The sliding doors are later additions and seem to match those used to blank off the exchange apparatus on TPO coaches – but this is definitely not one of the LNWR's Travelling Post Offices. The shame is that a) I couldn't get any closer to photograph it (I have a slightly better picture that didn't make the cut into this volume, but the coach is only visible at platform level and canopy supports intrude on the view), and b) I have no idea of its later fate, so I can't pick up the story later on. Perhaps some knowledgeable reader will be able to enlighten me.

RIGHT Here is a close-up of a rather fine bracket junction signal at the Wolverhampton end of Platform 7. It has two midget Starter arms (used in restricted spaces), and two Calling-on arms. The signal is guyed and the actuation rodding is clearly visible until it passes into a timber sleeve close to platform level. The rodding cranks at the foot of the signal are in a pit, boarded over for access.

ABOVE Here's a glorious little corner, with a platform bell push, probably to inform the signal box that a train is ready to depart; a telephone cabinet; a GWR 'Drinking Water' sign and a less-than-salubrious pair of taps to drink from (!); various bits of pipe and chain; and a hand-written notice for the guidance of parcels loading staff.

RIGHT Finally, a few details from around the station. The first is a contrast in trolleys, with an old wheelbarrow standing next to a modern BRUTE. Note the long-handled mop, the fire extinguisher cabinet, the window frames, the decorative corbels by the doorway and on the window hoods, and the window lights in the platform wall illuminating the passenger subway below, brought into use in 1903 following the underpinning and downwards extension of the station building.

So ends our venture into western parts. There are pictures of Wales, of course, but those are outside the scope of this volume. Our final chapter takes us back into more familiar territory.

Chapter Four

THE CENTRE OF ENGLAND

Our travels very rarely took us into the heart of the Midlands, which is ironic given that for various reasons that is where I've ended up living and working. In particular, Ted's later life brought him to the Midlands for employment reasons, none of which were connected with railways. The ironic thing is that if he had stayed with British Railways, after all the doubt about where the Signal & Telegraph Department might relocate to, it ended up in what was then called Stanier House in central Birmingham. I used to walk past this building on a daily basis, noting that it had one of the nameplates from the 'Duchess' Class locomotive No 46256 Sir William A. Stanier FRS on the wall of reception. At privatisation the building ceased to belong to British Rail and was taken over by W. S. Atkins in 2000. It was (somewhat inexplicably) renamed 'The Axis'.

There is still a cross-country line that currently has no passenger service, so rarely appears in writings about Midlands railways, and that's the line from Burton-on-Trent to Leicester. Part of the route included the original Leicester & Swannington Railway, but the Midland took it over in 1845 and expanded the line to serve the collieries in the area. In recent years the traffic has been more gravel and other aggregates; a lot of this now goes by road, and as a consequence the line is little used.

Passenger services ceased in 1964; British Rail was looking at restoring passenger traffic in the early 1990s, but these plans did not survive privatisation.

Coalville

Starting in 1978, open days were held at Coalville depot to raise funds for the St Christopher's Railway Orphanage in Derby, and these ran until 1991, the year the depot closed. Oddly, we never managed to get to Coalville until 1988, by which time these events were well established, with temporary passenger services, visiting steam and diesel locomotives and even quite high-profile engines visiting on rail tours. Passenger facilities were long gone (a temporary platform being erected to cope with the passenger services), but the goods shed survived, as did a proper Midland signal box and some depot buildings.

Coalville had at one time been a junction with a north-south route, the LNWR line from Nuneaton to Loughborough. Between Coalville and Nuneaton the line was actually jointly owned with the Midland Railway; nowadays, part of it survives between Shackerstone and Market Bosworth as 'The Battlefield Line'. Shackerstone station in particular has been nicely restored and, as one of Britain's less well-known heritage railways, is worth a visit.

LEFT This is the bridge over Mantle Lane itself, showing the relationship between the road, the signal box and the water tanks. The girder arrangement is notable, as is the vast amount of brickwork that went into such constructions. Crossing the bridge is 8F No 48151, one of the steam attractions at that year's Open Day. Owned by David Smith, this engine is still in operation at the time of writing and is based at Carnforth. It has since been named Gauge O Guild.

The other steam visitor that year was 'A4' Sir Nigel Gresley – appropriate, really, as five stations to the west along the line was (and still is) the town of Gresley. The Gresley family took the name when their ancestor, Nigel de Stafford, took the name of his castle in the area somewhere towards the end of the 11th century. They remained a powerful family until the family line died out in 1974; Sir Nigel was descended from a younger son who did not inherit the title, but nonetheless was from a well-off background. He attended Marlborough

College, but then went into railway engineering, serving his apprenticeship at Crewe before becoming a pupil of John Aspinall at Horwich Works; he then rose through the ranks on the Lancashire & Yorkshire Railway and moved to the Great Northern in 1911. The rest is history, though it would be difficult to imagine such a well-placed young man pursuing a similar career nowadays.

ABOVE This picture shows Coalville Mantle Lane signal box, with some depot buildings. The water tanks were a feature of Coalville for many years, though they were actually on the other side of Mantle Lane and not connected with the railway. There is a good worm's-eye view of an LMS-pattern ground signal, and some typical yard lamp-posts. Lots of blokes in high-visibility jerkins are about – we forget quite how long they've been a feature of the landscape, though the railways, with their emphasis on real health and safety, were early adopters.

Nuneaton

Talk of Nuneaton brings us closer to my adopted home territory. Nuneaton Trent Valley (as it was once known) has always been a major junction station, and indeed still is. In recent years additional platforms for Birmingham-Leicester trains have been added, but when I visited, first in 1980 for a depot Open Day in connection with the Rainhill Trials 150th anniversary, and then again in 1984, the station was still as it had been for many years.

Nuneaton station is a low brick building dating from 1915, the third station to serve on this site. It is generally undistinguished, apart from this clock tower, which conceals the staircase to the footbridge and a goods lift; in recent years this has been replaced by a passenger lift. There is some interesting detail around the clock pediment, which Gordon Biddle believes may identify this as the work of the LNWR architect Gerald Horsley.

The second photograph shows the interior of that footbridge; unusually the space was shared between pedestrians and parcels traffic, though the two were segregated by railings. These have now been removed, and the bridge extended to reach the new island Platforms 6 and 7. The Platform 2/3 buildings also date from 1915, but those on Platforms 4/5 date from the second iteration of the station in 1876.

LEFT A classic piece of railway furniture, the standard LNWR platform bench with its station name in the back was well-known to many well into the 1980s. We can also see some other familiar railway furniture here – the BR fluorescent light fitting with the station name emblazoned in it, the 'High speed trains pass this platform' notice (still in use in the first two decades of the 21st century), a BR litter bin and a Nestlé chocolate machine, which dispensed chocolate bars not otherwise known to the retail trade! One of my uncles had a job replenishing the similar machines on the London Underground, and he once told me that there was a scam being worked on them: if the stack of chocolate bars was arranged to jam, any money inserted into the machine while jammed was unrecoverable and a nice little earner for the person doing the refilling. And if you look closely, two of the stacks of chocolate bars in the machine seen here are completely full, and two are empty. (Interestingly, the similar machines I encountered in some out-of-the-way stations in rural Austria in the mid-1990s worked perfectly well, but they were visited so infrequently that the chocolate they contained was well past its sell-by date and had acquired a surface bloom from migrated sugars…)

BELOW This interesting relic, an LNWR-pattern bridge number plate, is of a type we have seen already at Whitchurch, but this one dates from BR times and the casting has been changed to reflect the new owners!

LEFT AND ABOVE These pictures show details of the canopy brackets at Nuneaton, and the maker's plate cast into one of the canopy supports. This appears to show that the latter, at least, were cast locally by a J. Williamson; 100 years of repainting has obscured the name sufficiently as to cast doubt on the company's second location – Wellington or Wellingborough?

RIGHT Here is some cast-iron evidence (literally!) of changing ownership, in the form of stop-tap covers cast by the LNWR and LMS espectively. Aspiring historians should always look around themselves in all directions, up and down as well as side to side…

BELOW Next we see the rather fine goods shed at Nuneaton, still emblazoned with the words 'London Midland and Scottish Railway Warehouse' at first-floor level across the end of the building. By 1980 the rails had been removed from the loading bays, and the whole building was being used to store rolls of material or insulation. There is a BR maroon totem 'No smoking' sign on the outer wall and a bell mounted on the end wall – a proper bell, not some electric contrivance! The goods office building has a bank of telephone insulators mounted on its end wall, something we have seen elsewhere. And there is a substantial timber hut in the picture, whose door bears the painted inscription 'Nuneaton Welders'.

RIGHT Meanwhile, local and cross-country services at Nuneaton were in the hands of first-generation DMUs. Here is a service for Birmingham New Street arriving in Platform 2 in the hands of a BRCW Class 118 three-car set. Notice the West Midlands PTE branding on the cab front; these sets were the mainstay of the Birmingham Cross-City line for many years, as well as handling many longer-distance services, especially once locomotive-hauled trains on the Birmingham-Leicester line were withdrawn in the late 1980s.

Nuneaton No 3 signal box is seen from the very end of Platform 5, looking north. This signal box was originally known as Nuneaton Down Sidings and was an LNWR Type 4 design, fitted with a 62-lever tumbler frame. It was reduced to a non-block post and redesignated Nuneaton Down Sidings Shunting Frame on 6 October 1963 when signalling passed to the Nuneaton power box upon the commissioning of colour light signalling. Prominent in the picture is a feeder for the overhead line gear and milepost 97, while in the distance can be seen the overbridge carrying the Midland avoiding line for direct Birmingham-Leicester trains. By this time it was used almost exclusively for freight; within a few years it would be first demolished then much later reinstated when the new Platforms 6 and 7 were introduced for Birmingham-Leicester services.

Water Orton

The WMPTE-branded DMU seen at Nuneaton would only have had one possible stop between Nuneaton and Birmingham, and that was a station with which I became very familiar between 1984 and about 2002 – Water Orton. I chose this as a station from which to commute into Birmingham, as it had a free council car park next door to it, and with no further stops between there and Birmingham it was a journey of 15 minutes – later reduced to 10 minutes when second-generation DMUs came into service. When I first knew Water Orton it was a staffed station most of the time; it had won 'Best Kept Station' awards in the late 1970s, and the waiting room was supplied with jigsaws and a small lending library by the station staff and village commuters. But providing a service to the travelling public costs money, and as

BR was prepared for privatisation first the staff were reduced to part-time, then were withdrawn, then the platform buildings were demolished without warning and a bus shelter provided – the glass in which lasted 24 hours before every single pane was broken. Then, with privatisation, the train service began to be cut back because Birmingham-Derby and Birmingham-Leicester services were potentially to be operated by two different franchises, so provision of a service at Water Orton was not a priority for whichever line a franchise was being offered for. Morning trains were eventually cut back until there was one train in the morning, at 7.50am, then nothing else until after 10.00am. The attitude of Central Trains, then the franchise-holder, appeared to be, 'We're fed up of telling people that there's no demand for this service,' while a West Midlands PTE bus ran parallel to the line (though it took a whole 50 minutes to get into Birmingham). The WMPTE franchise area for rail services ended at the county boundary about half a mile before the station, so WMPTE travel cards weren't valid on the trains at Water Orton, though they were on the buses – another trap for the unwary.

Eventually, a Parkway station was built at Coleshill (on the site of the old Forge Mills station), about two miles closer to Nuneaton, with a better service of trains (though not fantastically so) but higher fares, and a car park that (at the outset) cost £3.50 per day. By that time I'd given up on public transport and was driving into Birmingham, as the marginal cost of the additional

Here are some pictures of Water Orton in slightly happier times, although by the time these pictures were taken in 1985 and 1986 it was already long past its glory years, with the staffing cut to one part-timer. The first station on this site had been further to the east; this station was built in 1909, when the Midland opened the cut-off line that avoided Whitacre Junction (the original route survives as the 'Kingsbury Loop'). The passenger's first view of the station, from the bridge entrance, isn't all that imposing, although the station building itself is quite ornate, with pediments and decorative ironwork. On the left can be seen the separate luggage entry; ornate bridge parapets flank the entrance; and there are footings for a canopy over the entrance door (now no longer in place). This station building is often modelled, as plans appeared in one of the more prestigious model railway journals a few years ago; Midland Railway examples of overbridge entrance stations are fairly few and far between, making Water Orton an attractive prototype for modellers working with restricted areas (which is most of them!).

nine miles each way, plus the slightly higher parking fees, was outweighed by the additional convenience. Thus we see the dilemma of the public transport provider, especially when it has to charge a near economic price to run its service. (My nearest railway station is Birmingham International, but given the £8-per-day charge for the car park, plus the disruption to services in the event of any problem on the WCML, there are very few advantages to this option.)

Water Orton was the place where I used to encounter the last regional loco-hauled trains I can remember. For a while when I started commuting from there in 1984 my evening trains in particular were regularly hauled by Class 31s, often with up to seven coaches, and often including a Brake 1st. The idea of a regional cross-country semi-fast service having 1st Class accommodation is just unthinkable nowadays. The summer timetable of 1985 put a stop to this level of luxury, and from then on it was high-density DMUs such as we have already seen at Nuneaton. The picture I kick myself for never getting, though, was the morning Birmingham-Skegness service, which at around 7.40am

Once passengers had descended the stairway, they found themselves on the island platform with this range of timber buildings. They incorporated a waiting room (nearest the camera) with a separate ladies' waiting room and toilet; the gents' facilities were at the far end of the range of buildings. There is a large glazed canopy at the foot of the stairs, and two Midland-pattern platform benches are visible. This platform face was signalled for bi-directional working, with all trains between Leicester and Birmingham in both directions using this platform only; the junction had been moved closer to Birmingham some years before. You can also see the plant tubs and, halfway along the open platform, an enclosed flower bed that had been the local staff's contribution to the 'Best Kept Station' award.

called at Water Orton, and which was regularly hauled by a pair of Class 20s! For this reason Water Orton was often the haunt of 'gricers'; its junction location meant that there was a good assortment of traffic, and even today there are plenty of movements for those who like that sort of thing.

Way out

LEFT AND RIGHT Next we see a view of the back of the station building and the foot of the staircase. Some more flower tubs can be seen, attached to the timber of the staircase, and the gates for the goods lift are prominent. A facility like this was fairly uncommon at such a small station. The large brick extension behind the staircase housed the ticket office 'back room' at street level. Through the bridge can be seen the former Water Orton East Junction signal box, a BR structure put in place in the 1950s when its predecessor, a standard Midland signal box, was demolished by a freight train derailment. By this time the building seen here was no longer in use as a signal box, but as a PW store; it was accessed by the doorway directly under the footbridge, passing through the station basement and then through the timbered-in central arch of the road bridge, as clearances under the rail section of the bridge were too tight on both sides to allow foot passage.

BELOW Here is the East Junction box itself (there was, of course, a West Junction box, serving the extensive marshalling yard, the junction for the Midland line via Sutton Coldfield to Walsall, and the private sidings for Birmingham Corporation's extensive Minworth sewage farm and its narrow-gauge internal network). There is a fine collection of huts; working from left to right, the first carries a warning sign alerting PW staff to the bi-directional nature of the line at this point; then there is a rather derelict LMS lamp hut; then a concrete toilet hut and a ballast bin; then the signal box coal bunker, with a safety rail between it and the box proper to discourage staff from stepping out towards the running lines. On the other side of the down line are further stores, including a propane store for the gas bottles used for temporary speed restriction signs and other PW purposes; these are also protected by a railing. The Church Lane footbridge, a fine Midland structure, was provided to maintain the public right of way when the new railway severed Church Lane itself at this point. In the mist in the background can be seen the landmark cooling towers of Hams Hall C power station, which were to last until 1993. Hams Hall B is over to the left slightly; the cooling towers had probably only been demolished a short time before this picture was taken in November 1985, though the chimneys just visible to the left of the trees remained until 1988.

Banbury

But away with all the depressing dereliction and neglect at Water Orton! Let's look at somewhere with much more interest, and a station that still looks substantially similar now to when I photographed it in 1975 – Banbury.

Banbury is one of the most distinctive stations on the GWR Oxford-Birmingham line, and it is pleasing to report that it has been renovated and kept substantially unchanged by Chiltern Rail. That is not to say that it is some red-brick, glass and timber monument; instead, it is a rather unusual example of a large provincial station rebuilt between 1956 and 1958 – firmly in the concrete era but before the period of system-build. The clean lines of the building are evident; this is from a time where new materials didn't mean shoddy design or workmanship. In 1958 this station must have been the epitome of modernity. Banbury had been listed for rebuilding by the GWR in 1937, using £167,250 from the Government Guaranteed Loans scheme, partly with the aim of creating a new joint station with the LNER (which had a branch off the Great Central main line) and the LMS (in the form of the old LNWR Merton Street station, with services to Towcester and Bletchley, which by the mid-1930s was a rather antiquated

affair), but also intended to ease the curve and increase line speeds through the station area to 75mph. The intervening hostilities and nationalisation delayed the work for some 20 years, but improvements were made before the war to the goods facilities and offices.

The first view is taken looking south from the road overbridge. The station is a very clean design, and just look at all those neat and empty platforms, including bays for the Great Central services to Woodford Halse (including the disused platform face on the left of the picture). There's a goodly selection of parcels vans waiting for traffic, too. To the left of the station can be seen the goods avoiding lines, and what was to evolve into a stabling point. On the extreme left can be seen some cattle pens, then a coal yard and, beyond that, more cattle pens. Out of shot to the left is a new building occupying the site of the yard that separated the GWR station from the LNWR Merton Street station, which closed to passengers in 1961 and to goods in 1966. The second set of cattle pens, near the gas works, were put in by BR with the rebuilding of the station, primarily because Banbury was home to Western Europe's largest cattle market, whose site was actually on Merton Street; that closed in 1998.

ABOVE Next, some views of the north end of the station. First we see a view from the Bridge Street bridge, with Banbury North box prominent. At the time of writing Banbury remains one of the few places where there are still semaphore signals; given Network Rail's intention to eliminate manual signal boxes, these cannot be long for this world. Banbury had a mix of semaphore and colour lights when the station was remodelled in 1958, and it is interesting to note that although the station was by now in London Midland Region territory, GWR-pattern lower-quadrant signals were used, most likely because putting in standard LMS/BR-pattern upper-quadrants would have also meant remodelling the entire signalling installation, and Banbury had two 87-lever boxes to contend with. But even in 1975 two operational boxes and a set of GWR-type signals were rather unusual, especially for a dyed-in-the-wool Derby lad.

Between the box and the road bridge is the BR relay room, again part of the 1958 rebuilding, and housing the necessary equipment for the colour light signals and any power-operated points. Beyond the box is what looks like a small bothy, to judge by the chimney. The two Banbury boxes were built in 1908, though their frames were updated in November 1944.

LEFT A closer look at one of the GWR lower-quadrant signals – this one controlled one of the bay platforms, not the main line! There is also a station clock and one of the concrete lamp-posts in this shot.

ABOVE This is Banbury South signal box, which was also built in 1908 but, unlike the North box, has an internal staircase.

BELOW Finally a look at the goods shed, which was part of the early improvement works done by the GWR in 1937. There is a small two-lever frame in the foreground, controlling entry to the goods shed roads. Note the venerable GWR vans on the siding at the rear, including an 'Iron Mink', and there is a BR 'Door-to-Door' container grounded behind the parked cars; the latter, by the way, are all British – Fords, Vauxhalls and Austins.

Moreton-in-Marsh

Moreton-in-Marsh is a picturesque town on the old Fosse Way and on the northern edge of the Cotswolds. But in railway terms it was once part of one of the true horror stories of the Railway Mania, the period of intense railway speculation and planning that came about in the years after the successful opening of the pioneer lines. Like the dot-com bubble of our time, many companies were proposed, launched, begun, suspended, abandoned, absorbed and forgotten, while their promoters either became monstrously rich or went completely bust – and quite often both, in quick succession. Moreton-in-Marsh had been one end of the Stratford-upon-Avon & Moreton Tramway, a horse-drawn wagonway between those two towns, opened in 1821 to transport coal from the terminus of the Stratford-on-Avon Canal into the rural heartland of southern Warwickshire, and to return agricultural produce and minerals northwards and thence to distant markets.

A branch from Moreton to Shipston-on-Stour was built in 1836. Only nine years later a Parliamentary Act was passed for a line with greater ambitions, the Oxford, Worcester & Wolverhampton Railway. But this didn't change the situation of the tramway for some time, as the OWW, despite being backed by the GWR, could neither raise sufficient capital for its construction, nor manage its affairs sufficiently well so as to be able to get traffic moving on even that part of the line it did manage to build, with the effect that it took seven years to get even 36 miles of route built, from Stoke Junction (south of Bromsgrove on the Midland line), via Worcester to Evesham. In another year the line was completed through Moreton to Wolvercote Junction, outside Oxford, and although this line continued to be troublesome in terms of railway politics, at least goods could begin to move along it and traders could now find outlets in Worcester, and get their goods there more quickly than the tramway ever managed. The tramway tried to move with the times and experimented with steam traction, but this required more investment than the traffic could generate. In 1859 the section from Moreton to Shipston was converted to a conventional railway, but the tramway went bankrupt in 1868 and was acquired by the GWR, which was consolidating its activities, having acquired the OWW – by this time known generally as 'the Old Worse and Worse' – outright in 1861.

All this history has a bearing on the station, layout and structures at Moreton.

The first picture shows the station building from the road side. This may have been designed by W. G. Owen and dates from 1873. It is a fairly plain building, but nicely finished in yellow brick with red-brick banding. The timber porch is not original. Note that there is an external telephone bell mounted on the telegraph pole, and a Ford Cortina Mk II and a Renault 6 have pulled up to the impressive run of GWR cast-iron fencing that separates the forecourt from the station platform.

ABOVE Moreton-in-Marsh Signal Box dates from 1883, and is slightly unusual in that it not only has the normal point rodding out-run at the front, but also has one at the side. The 40-lever frame here dates from 1911. Also in this picture you can see a dustbin, a phone cabinet, the planking arrangement for the oblique barrow crossing and a guy post for the box's terminal telegraph pole. And note the concrete lamp standard on the left of the picture – a standard Southern Railway-pattern station lamp. Obviously BR didn't feel the need to produce a completely new design of concrete lamp standard in the 1950s, and the Southern's expertise in precast concrete must have been appreciated enough to continue to use its pattern beyond the confines of the Southern Region. Running behind the box is a set of lines that originally formed the Shipston-on-Stour branch; this closed to freight in 1960, but this section was retained as useful stabling sidings.

BELOW The next picture shows the platform side of the station building. Of note are the three platform barrows, the typical GWR platform seats, a very neatly clipped hedge, and the goodly selection of posters and advertising boards. Sadly, the building has lost its chimneys.

This is the view from the footbridge looking back towards Oxford. The sidings on the left of the picture are the rump of the Shipston-on-Stour branch. There is a fine array of GWR platform seats on the up platform, and the Southern-pattern lamp standards are now more visible. The goods shed can be seen to the right of the running lines; it is a mean little structure that replaced the earlier Brunel-designed one on this site. We can see the back of a GWR lower-quadrant signal in the 'six foot', which is the Inner Home for Worcester-bound trains using the down platform, the line having been singled in 1971. Signalling the down platform line for bi-directional working would mean that the station could continue to work if the up line was blocked through shunting movements. Network Rail has recently reinstated the double track, though this is rather too late for wagonload freight.

Evesham

Further along the OWW was Evesham. This justified a larger station than Moreton, and we see it here from the road overbridge, looking north-west towards Worcester. The overall layout can be seen here; the station must have been doing a roaring trade in parcels, as there were six platform trolleys on the station when I visited, one of them electric! In 1956 parcels through Evesham amounted to 143,000 dispatched and 49,000 received; 20 years later this still seemed to be a major trade. Just off the picture to the left was a former weighbridge hut being used as a taxi office, and beyond that on the other side of the forecourt was the former Midland station.

On the right of the picture is a loading bay, with substantial retaining walls and a ramp giving road access to the loading area. This does not appear to ever have been a platform road, given that the platform building is built up to the platform edge and there is fencing along the back edge of the platform on both sides of the building.

The station boasts a good number of GWR-pattern platform seats; on many of them the GWR 'button' logo can clearly be seen on the support castings. This pattern of seat lasted a long time, and was continued even after nationalisation except that instead of 'GWR' the supports read 'BR (W)'. Truly was it said that at nationalisation Britain's railways were divided into five regions and the Great Western!

Next we see the station building. The family likeness to that at Moreton-in-Marsh can be seen, but this station has survived better with its chimneys intact. It also boasts a substantial canopy, though this is no longer glazed, unfortunately. There is a (locally-produced?) police 'No Parking' sign outside the booking office, and a Midland Red timetable board on the wall (next to the bicycle). As with Moreton, there is liberal provision of GWR cast-iron fencing. Sadly, the original doors to the booking office have been replaced by modern full-length glazed doors; the parcels office doors further along the building give a better impression of what was possibly there before.

Next is a view of the platform side of the main building. For
a provincial small town station there was, as I remember, quite
a lot of bustle about it and the staff were certainly keeping
busy. The hanging baskets are evidence of the sort of care not
normally found today. Again, the fleet of trolleys is very evident,
including the electric one. And if more evidence is needed of the
amount of parcels traffic being handled, there is a prominent set
of modern Pooley luggage scales on the platform – something
I never saw anywhere else. I saw old, disused ones, of course,
but never such a modern piece of kit as this. And look carefully
– although they have carrying wheels, the scales are mounted on
their own little plinth. The scales had a capacity of 100kg (don't
forget that the UK started to go metric in 1965!), making them

quite a substantial item. The two platform seats make an
interesting contrast; that nearer the camera is the standard
example, as described earlier, but the one further away is a type
designed by the GWR but intended for use in booking office
halls and waiting rooms. With the passage of time, many of
these got moved outside, but their ornate end arms give them
away. Above the nearer seat can be seen that station clock;
it was possible to see where the GWR 'button' logo on the clock
face had been applied over earlier lettering, meaning that it
was in situ in 1934 when that logo was introduced. In the
background is the Railway Hotel; the wording along its
balustrade is quite old, to judge by the typeface and the
use of a full stop in a piece of signwriting.

The building on the opposite platform boasts hanging baskets and two 'indoor' GWR benches. And at the foot of the footbridge steps (just out of shot to the left) there is a handy map of the London Underground; obviously the station master was used to thinking of his passengers and considering their needs when they got to 'that London'!

Finally, we take a look at the Midland station, which closed in 1963. This line had been built in 1864 and was part of a long route that left the Midland at Barnt Green and meandered across country until it rejoined the main line at Ashchurch. From 1931 both the MR (by now, LMS) and GWR stations were put under the control of the LMS station master. Interestingly, although the station had been closed for 13 years when this picture was taken, there was still a British Railways notice board on its wall, and its posters had been updated with the current campaigns! There is also an interesting poster for the 'Birmingham shopping centre', 'above New Street station'

– this, of course, was rebranded a number of times, most recently as 'The Pallasades' (perhaps best not to probe into the spelling of that too closely), and is, at the time of writing, under sentence of death as part of the redevelopment of New Street, to be replaced with something ultra-modern and far more attractive – something that was probably in the minds of the original architect when New Street was first redeveloped in the 1960s… There is a grand collection of 1970s motoring parked here: from left to right, they are a Ford Cortina Mk III estate, a Saab 99, a Citroen DS, a Rover 3500 and a Morris Marina. At least three of these cars would be considered highly desirable today!

Gloucester

To end with, here is a visit to Gloucester. Gloucester station has as convoluted a history as anywhere else, and boasts the country's second longest platform (1,977 feet, or nearly 603 metres). (Since you ask, the longest is at Colchester – 2,034 feet, or 620 metres.) The current station is on the site of the original joint station shared by the Birmingham & Gloucester Railway and the Cheltenham & Great Western Union Railway, and since changed into a through station for onward trains along the west bank of the Severn Estuary to Newport. Other railway development meant that this station was served by a triangular junction off the main Birmingham-Bristol line, forcing any through trains to or from Bristol and Birmingham to reverse if they call here. Later, the Midland decided to build a separate line into Gloucester to achieve its own independent route to the town, and in 1896 built its own station, later known as Gloucester Eastgate, linked to the existing (now solely GWR) station by a 250-yard-long covered footbridge. Unfortunately, that line ended up with five level crossings, causing great disruption to traffic in the town, so in 1975 it was decided to rationalise the situation by closing Eastgate and rebuilding the existing Gloucester station (then known as Gloucester Central). The accompanying pictures were taken in 1976, halfway through the redevelopment process.

The first picture is looking west from towards the end of Platform 1, the closest point to Cheltenham. From here, it's possible to get some idea of the physical length of the platform at Gloucester. It was designed with the intention that it could accept two full HST sets at the same time. In the centre is the parcels platform, built in 1914; dedicating this platform to parcels traffic instead of passengers was one of the major changes made with the 1975-77 reconstruction. Gloucester was a major parcels hub; the goods shed right of centre was re-dedicated wholly to parcels traffic at this time. No 08 825 was one of two shunters working hard around that station when I visited.

ABOVE The second picture is taken from about halfway along the platform. The crossover allowing trains to access Platform 2 while Platform 1 is occupied is in the centre of the picture. You will see that there are GWR-pattern platform seats on the extreme left, retained from the old station. In the centre of the picture is the 1914 platform, and this view shows how many parcels trolleys and BRUTEs were involved in the movement of that traffic.

FACING PAGE The last picture shows the closed Eastgate station. The site of the former covered footbridge was still visible when this picture was taken (though none of the remains are on this picture). And indeed, the station building was still occupied and rails were still in situ.

It's odd to think that in so many cases what I have photographed has since been altered or even swept away through later changes. In some of these pictures railway staff can be seen going about their everyday tasks, although I did try to avoid getting too much in their way or making my photography too obvious. We were only really challenged once by an over-zealous official – another example of how things have changed between Then and Now. But in the course of assembling this book and examining these pictures again for the first time in many years, I have from time to time spotted a few railwaymen keeping a beady eye on Ted and me, just making sure that we were not up to no good and, in the odd instance, making sure they were in the picture.

It must have been nice to think that complete strangers were interested in what you did for a living; there can be very few jobs these days where that can be true. But isn't that what an interest in railways is about? An appreciation of the work of untold thousands of people, leaving something behind that future generations will use and enjoy, and that will help their lives. In 1976 Peter Gray, then the works manager of the Derby Carriage & Wagon Works in Litchurch Lane, wrote this in his foreword to the centenary brochure prepared for that year's Open Day: '…in many ways we are enjoying the fruits of the labours of those who went before us. We must see that what we leave will be as constructive as what we inherited.'

Afterword

And so we reach the end of this exploration of Britain's railway history through the physical evidence of the structures and artefacts the steam age left behind. There is certainly more where this came from – pictures from the East Midlands, from North and Mid Wales, from the Northern Fells and the West Country, from Yorkshire and from Tyneside.

A work like this is only as good as the research I have been able to do, and the Bibliography is a guide to the sources I have consulted. In recent years the Internet has been both a boon and a trap for researchers; sometimes what one finds there has to be carefully cross-checked with other sources, but the websites I have listed are the ones that have been most useful to me. My thanks go out to all those people, named and unnamed, who have given their time and effort for free so that people anywhere in the world can share their knowledge.

Any errors in the text are mine alone. I am always happy to be corrected or to have my knowledge expanded, so if any readers can spot something where they know better than me about some fact or opinion, please feel free to contact me. My e-mail address is robertday154@talktalk.net; those of you who prefer to put real pen to real paper should write to me care of the publishers.

My thanks go to Peter Waller and Nick Grant, my editors at Ian Allan, and to my good friend Cathy, who gave me encouragement and praise, and some urging to get back to work when that was what was needed instead of mere ego massage.

There are many railway staff and members of the public appearing in these pictures; if any recognises themselves, please feel free to get in touch. (I recently found myself in a crowd picture taken at the Tramway Museum in Crich one August Bank Holiday, and I appear in the background of a J. Arthur Dixon postcard of the LNWR engine Hardwicke at York.) Railways are ultimately about people, the people who work for them and the people who travel on them; it is important that people play a part in these pictures.

Bibliography

Anderson, P. Howard *Forgotten Railways: The East Midlands* (Newton Abbot: David & Charles, 1973)

Banks, Chris *The Birmingham to Leicester Line* (Sparkford: Haynes/Oxford Publishing Co, 1994) *British Railways Past and Present 23: Nottinghamshire and Derbyshire* (Wadenhoe: Past and Present Publishing, 1996)

Barman, Christian *Next Station* (London: Great Western Railway, 1946)

Barnes, E. G. *The Midland Main Line* (London: George Allen & Unwin, 1969)

Batty, Stephen R. *Rail Centres: Sheffield* (Shepperton: Ian Allan, 1984)

Beard, Andrew 'Shrewsbury: at the crossroads' in *British Railways Illustrated Annual No 1* (Pinner: Irwell Press, 1992)

Belper Historical Society *Belper: a study of its history based on visual evidence* (Belper: the Society, 1970)

Bendall, Ian R. *Industrial Locomotives of Nottinghamshire* (London: Industrial Railway Society, 1999)

Bentley, Ben 'Severn Bridge Junction' (*Shropshire Star*, 11 April 2012)

Bentley, J. M. *The Railway from Buxton to Bakewell, Matlock & Ambergate* (Romiley: Foxline Publishing, 1989)

Bentley, J. M. and Fox, G. K. *Railways of the High Peak; Buxton to Ashbourne* (Scenes from the Past No 32) (Romiley: Foxline Publishing, 1997)

Biddle, Gordon *Britain's Historic Railway Buildings: A gazetteer of structures and sites* (Hersham: Ian Allan, 2011)

Billson, Peter *Derby and the Midland Railway* (Derby: Breedon Books, 1996)

British Railways, London Midland Region. Sectional Appendix to Working Timetable and books of rules and regulations: Midland lines (Derby: British Railways, October 1960)

Special notice 998G: Notice to drivers, guards, signalmen and others respecting the resignalling between Nuneaton Ashby Junction and Brinklow, and between Nuneaton and Weddington Junction, Abbey Junction, Griff Junction and Midland Junction (Crewe: British Railways, October 1963)

British Transport Commission (Railway Clearing House): Official hand-book of stations (etc.) (London: British Transport Commission [Railway Clearing House], 1956)

Christiansen, Rex *A Regional History of the Railways of Great Britain, Volume 7: The West Midlands* (Newton Abbot: David & Charles, 1983 [second, revised edition])

Daniels, Gerald and Dench, L. A. *Passengers No More* (Shepperton: Ian Allan, 1973 [second edition])

Dixey, S. John 'Charles Trubshaw: A Victorian railway architect' in Jenkinson, David (editor) *Bedside BackTrack: Aspects of Britain's railway history* (Penryn: Atlantic Transport Publishers, 1993)

Dow, George *Great Central, Volume I: The Progenitors, 1813-1863* (London: Locomotive Publishing Company, 1959 [second impression, 1966]) *Midland Style* (Bromley: Historical Model Railway Society, 1975)

Dunstan, John *The Origins of the Sheffield and Chesterfield Railway* (Dore: Dore Village Society, 1970)

Ellis, C. Hamilton *The Midland Railway* (Ashford: Malaga Books, 1966)

Forster, Vic and Taylor, Bill *Railways in and around Nottingham* (Scenes from the Past No 11) (Stockport: Foxline Publishing, 1991)

Glover, John *British Electric Trains in Camera* (Shepperton: Ian Allan, 1982)

Hardy, Clive *Derbyshire Railways* (Stroud: Sutton Publishing, 1997)

Henshaw, Alfred *The Great Northern Railway in the East Midlands: The Erewash Valley lines, Pinxton branch, Awsworth-Ilkeston, Heanor & Stanton branches* (Sawtry: Railway Correspondence & Travel Society, 2000)

Hudson, Bill *Through Limestone Hills: The Peak Line, Ambergate-Chinley* (Sparkford: Haynes/Oxford Publishing Co, 1989)

Kaye, David *British Bus Fleets 5: East Midlands* (Shepperton: Ian Allan, 1965)

Leleux, Robin *A Regional History of the Railways of Great Britain, Volume 9: The East Midlands* (Newton Abbot: David & Charles, 1976)

London, Midland & Scottish Railway Company. General Appendix to the Working Time Tables, with Sectional Appendix: Midland Division (Derby: the company, March 1937)

Maund, R. *Passenger Train Services over Unusual Lines* (Private publication, 2008)

Nock, O. S. *The Great Western Railway in the Nineteenth Century* (London: Ian Allan, 1962)

Perkins, C. J. and Padgett, R. *The Midland Railway in Nottingham, Volume II, 1908-1947: Decades of Change* (Nottingham: the authors, 2001) *Volume III, 1948-1999: From Steam to Diesel* (Nottingham: the authors, 2002)

Pixton, Bob *North Midland: Portrait of a famous route, Part One, Derby to Chesterfield* (Cheltenham: Runpast Publishing, 2000)

Radford, J. B. (Brian) *A Century of Progress: Centenary brochure of the Derby Carriage and Wagon Works* (Derby: British Rail Engineering, 1977) *Derby Works and Midland Locomotives* (Shepperton: Ian Allan, 1971) *Midland Through the Peak: A pictorial history of the Midland Railway main line routes between Derby and Manchester* (Paddock Wood: Unicorn Books, 1988) *Rail Centres: Derby* (Shepperton: Ian Allan, 1986)

Railway Clearing House: Hand-book of stations (etc.) (Newton Abbot: David & Charles, 1970 [reprint of first edition, 1904])

Sprenger, Howard *Rails to Ripley* (Southampton: Kestrel Railway Books, 2009)

Stamp, Gavin *Telephone Boxes* (London: Chatto & Windus, 1989)

Talbot, Edward et al *LNWR Liveries* (Southwold: Historical Model Railway Society, 1985)

Tuffrey, Peter *Nottingham's Railways: From the Bill Reed collection* (Stroud: Chalford Publishing, 1997)

Vanns, Michael A. *Rail Centres: Nottingham* (Shepperton: Ian Allan, 1993) *Signalling in the Age of Steam* (Shepperton: Ian Allan, 1995)

Vaughan, Adrian *A Pictorial Record of Great Western Architecture* (Poole: Oxford Publishing Company, 1977)

Walkerdine, R. H. and Corbin, E. G. (editors) *Guide to the Coalfields, 1957* (London: The Colliery Guardian, 1957)

Warburton, L. G. *A Pictorial Record of LMS Signals* (Oxford: Oxford Publishing Co., 1972)

Williams, F. S. *The Midland Railway: Its Rise and Progress* (Newton Abbot: David & Charles, 1968] reprint of 5th edition, 1876])

Journals, etc

House of Commons Hansard
Ripley and Heanor News
Shropshire Star
The House Magazine
The Independent

Websites

http://www.6lda28.com/brel/index.html – Derby Locomotive works
http://www.britishlistedbuildings.co.uk/en-469008-footbridge-to-north-of-whitchurch-railwa
http://derbyshire.greatbritishlife.co.uk/article/riber-castle--life-at-the-top-37240/
http://www.disused-stations.org.uk/b/buxton/index.shtml – Nick Catford. Disused stations; closed railway
     stations of the UK – Buxton (Midland)
http://www.disused-stations.org.uk/w/whitchurch/index.shtml – Paul Wright. Disused stations; closed railway
     stations of the UK – Whitchurch
http://dspace.dial.pipex.com/town/square/ca14/ALYCIDON%20RAIL/Electrification%20archive/
     Electrification%20review%201981%20revisited%20May%202006.htm – a retrospective of the 1981
     Government study of future rail electrification proposals
http://www.derby-signalling.org.uk/Station.htm – David Harris. Signalling around Derby station
http://www.forgottenrelics.co.uk/routes/butterley1.html – Simon Swain. Butterley – Langley Mill railway
http://www.greatwestern.org.uk/stat_1.htm, *.*/stat_4.htm – John Daniel. The Great Western archive; a selection
     of Great Western stations
http://www.heritage-explorer.co.uk/web/he/searchdetail.aspx?id=10248&crit=&pid=60
     and http://viewfinder.english-heritage.org.uk/search/reference.
     aspx?uid=15900&index=0&mainQuery=shrewsbury&searchType=all&form=home – English heritage.
     Howard Street warehouse, Shrewsbury
http://www.localhistory.scit.wlv.ac.uk/articles/railways/S%20and%20B.htm – Oakengates station
http://www.lwmrs.co.uk/CMS/index.php/members-layouts/98-ambergate-em/145-ambergate-em – Nick
     Meredith. Ambergate – EM/P4
http://www.railblue.com/index.htm – a comprehensive guide to BR diesels of the 'Rail Blue' era
http://www.roscalen.com/signals/Shrewsbury/index.htm – Adrian 'the Rock'. Signals at Shrewsbury
http://www.warwickshirerailways.com/gwr/moreton_marsh.htm – Mike Musson
http://en.wikipedia.org/wiki/Derby_railway_station
http://en.wikipedia.org/wiki/Derby_Works
http://en.wikipedia.org/wiki/Gloucester_railway_station
http://en.wikipedia.org/wiki/Gresley_Baronets
http://en.wikipedia.org/wiki/Hams_Hall_power_stations
http://en.wikipedia.org/wiki/National_Shell_Filling_Factory,_Chilwell
http://en.wikipedia.org/wiki/Nigel_Gresley
http://en.wikipedia.org/wiki/Sheffield_station
http://en.wikipedia.org/wiki/Stratford_and_Moreton_Tramway
http://en.wikipedia.org/wiki/Totley_Tunnel
http://en.wikipedia.org/wiki/Woodhead_Tunnel
http://railways.national-preservation.com/steam-traction/22588-dinting-railway-centre.html
– a discussion group on Dinting, with contributions from those who tried unsuccessfully to save the site for re-
     preservation in 2011.
http://sites.google.com/site/pacerchaser/railway-pages/train-pages--hull-and-east-riding-railways-part-1--trains-
     in-the-80-s-and-90-s – 'Pacerchaser'. Train Pages – Hull and East Riding Railways part 1- Trains in the 80's
     and 90's – some possible evidence for the coaches I saw being attached to cross-country services in the 1970s at
     Sheffield possibly being Hull – Brighton through coaches